FROM *Society Page*
TO **Front Page**
NEBRASKA WOMEN IN JOURNALISM

★ ★ EILEEN M. WIRTH ★ ★

UNIVERSITY OF NEBRASKA PRESS | LINCOLN & LONDON

To Don —
My compatriot of all
these years. I hope you enjoy
this.   Eileen Wirth

© 2013 by the Board of Regents of the University
of Nebraska. All rights reserved. Manufactured in
the United States of America. ∞
Publication of this volume was assisted by a grant
from the Friends of the University of Nebraska
Press.

Library of Congress Cataloging-in-Publication Data
Wirth, Eileen M., 1947–
From society page to front page: Nebraska women
in journalism / Eileen M. Wirth.
pages cm
Includes bibliographical references.
ISBN 978-0-8032-3293-8 (pbk: alk. paper)
1. Women journalists—Nebraska—Biography.
2. Journalism—Nebraska—History—20th century.
I. Title.
PN4872.W56 2013
070.408209782—dc23   2012043716

Set in Minion Pro by Laura Wellington.
Designed by A. Shahan.

In memory of my dad, Austin Wirth,
who ordered me to take a journalism class,
and to my professional mentors,
the late Wilma Crumley and Mary McGrath

Contents

ILLUSTRATIONS

Following page 90

Preface

This book about the first century of Nebraska women in journalism is for everyone who helped open opportunities to women in any field. It's also for younger people who want to know more about what Mom and Grandma went through to create opportunities for them and for those who simply like good stories about colorful women. The women in this book were suffragists, "flapper journalists," White House correspondents, war correspondents, Rosie the Reporters, local publishers, and pioneers in broadcasting. Some roamed the globe covering the Russian Revolution and the Vietnam War, while others made their impact on small Nebraska towns. Although only Willa Cather is a household name, you'll meet memorable women such as a 102-year-old columnist, members of a wire service bureau in World War II who agreed to be fired at its end, and the editor of a major suffragist newspaper published in Beatrice, Nebraska.

When I began researching this book, friends elsewhere kiddingly asked if there was anything to write about. Initially I wasn't sure because media history focuses on the national rather than the local and even national women get limited attention. However, as I dug through a myriad of sources, I was amazed at the treasures I found. As I completed my first draft, a Wisconsin colleague in women's history expressed envy at my wealth of subjects to cover, including Willa Cather, Clara Bewick Colby, Rheta Childe Dorr, Bess Furman, Marianne Means, and others.

I undertook this study because I teach media history at Creighton University, and I participated in the integration of women into city news at the *Omaha World-Herald*, where I was a reporter from 1969 to 1980. Like many of my contemporaries, I was angry about the sexism and ageism that surfaced in the coverage of Hillary Clinton's 2008 presidential campaign. It seemed to disregard and disrespect my generation of women and our struggles for equal opportunity. It hit me that most of our efforts were quiet, local, and all but invisible even to our coworkers although the national struggles for equality had been highly publicized. I could not recall ever reading anything about the integration of women into local media in the 1970s and decided to tell this story.

Then Heather Lundine of the University of Nebraska Press offered a greater challenge. Instead of focusing just on the baby boomers, she told me to research Nebraska's women journalists from the 1870s to the 1970s. What a revelation! I discovered that we boomers were merely a link in a chain of amazing women going back to the Victorian era. These historic stories begged to be told and placed in context — a mission that I became even more passionate about after speaking to a group of older women at the Loyola University School of Communication in Chicago. After the talk, many shared memories that my stories had evoked, including a Peabody Award winner whose employer had hidden her from clients to keep them from realizing that a woman was working on their accounts. These women couldn't even challenge employers who advertised for "attractive" single women and fired them if they married or became pregnant. It reinforced my conviction that the women of the Nebraska press really do epitomize legions of women everywhere who sought a fuller life. I hope that many will be inspired to tell their own stories.

SIGNIFICANCE OF THE PROJECT

We cannot fully understand the history of American media without studying regional and local journalism because that's where the bulk of journalists have worked, but most texts focus on national events and figures. The history of women in local media is especially spotty. I hope that the light this project sheds on women journalists in a typical "flyover" state suggests the riches that other researchers might find in their areas. Maurine Beasley, one of the nation's leading experts on women in media history, told me in a phone interview that she is unaware of any similar longitudinal examination of women journalists in a single state. The fact that it produced such interesting results should encourage other researchers to adopt this research model.

My goal has been to write a historically accurate book aimed at general readers and students. Uncovering this history has been challenging because my sources were extremely scattered and many were not available online. Because there is limited material on many of the women I describe, full profiles were impossible to write, but the short segments flesh out the historical record. The bibliographic essay details my full research path and myriad of sources consulted, but I feel part of the importance of this book is that it pulls together unrelated pieces of information that collectively provide insights into the history of both Nebraska women and Nebraska journalism, thus preserving them for the state historical record.

This project also demonstrates the value of interviewing major figures in local journalism history to record their memories before it is too late. Several of my most helpful sources were over eighty, and at least three have died since our interviews. Much of the information in this book could never have been captured without the assistance of these journalistic veterans because the stories they shared can't be Googled.

PLAN OF THE BOOK

This book is organized chronologically except for a chapter on three giants of early Nebraska journalism: Elia Peattie, Willa Cather, and Clara Bewick Colby. There's also a chapter on women of color in Nebraska journalism that cuts across several decades. I conclude with a chapter on the integration of women into

Omaha journalism in the 1970s and its results. The epilogue reflects briefly on the project. Chapters begin with historical scene setting then tell the stories of women from each period in addition to covering such things as pay, working conditions, and journalism education.

I conclude most chapters by analyzing samples of articles by and about women from the general and social news sections. Newspaper coverage of mundane local events often reveals more about how people lived than political history. I focus on coverage of women in the major Omaha and Lincoln papers because they circulated throughout the state, especially the *Omaha World-Herald*. Many of the articles are like family stories of life in "the olden days."

Writing styles and story selections changed from decade to decade, and they offer wonderful insights into life and journalism in the various eras. I have paid particular attention to story selections because editors assign articles on topics that concern readers. The language used to describe women is important because it provided a lens through which contemporary readers viewed women and especially the way that women were socialized to view themselves. In most cases the issues examined are fairly random and thus hopefully typify the way contemporary media depicted women.

One challenge of writing a book on women is that their last names change with their marital status. Whenever possible I give the maiden and the married name on first reference and use whichever makes the most sense for a given period in a woman's life on second reference, but total consistency is impossible.

A FINAL NOTE

The bulk of my Creighton journalism students have been women, and I have always been saddened that they know so little about what it took to open this field to them. I hope this book enriches their understanding of the contributions of women to journalism so that they will be inspired to emulate these women. This book is my gift to them as well as to my children, grandchildren, nieces, and nephews. Finally, I hope readers will love these women and learn from their achievements. Laugh, marvel, and enjoy! Be moved and inspired.

Acknowledgments

I could not have written this book without the help of a great many people, including everyone I interviewed and those who led me to them, people who assisted me with research, and close friends who supported me through the process. Names of interviewees are listed in the bibliography, but a number of people deserve special thanks.

My sister, Janet Poley, suggested that I write about Nebraska women in journalism and offered numerous helpful suggestions in addition to being a constant cheerleader. Thanks, Jan!

Allen Beermann of the Nebraska Press Association and Patricia Gaster and Andrea Faling of the Nebraska State Historical Society guided me to sources and stories that I would never otherwise have found. I deeply appreciate their vast knowledge and their willingness to share it. Larry Walklin of the University of Nebraska College of Journalism was my primary source for information about historic women in broadcasting. Amy Forss of Metropolitan Community College generously shared her research on Nebraska's African American press and Mildred Brown. Mary Nash, Creighton University's peerless reference librarian, not only located a great deal of information for me but acted as if it were fun, which was typical of the entire staff of Reinert Alumni Library. My research assistant, Kyle McGinn, patiently verified references and formatted them properly. My administrative assistant Nichole Jelinek helped with countless computer tasks.

Although I quote Cornelia Flora of Iowa State University only sparingly, her insights into the sociology of midwestern women provided a framework for all the stories, especially the changes of the 1960s. Beatrice Public Library director Laureen Riedesel provided references and background on Clara Bewick Colby that aided my understanding of not only Colby but also the suffragist movement.

Much of the fun in doing this book was reconnecting with veterans of Nebraska journalism and others who not only shared their memories and confirmed or clarified oral history tales but suggested leads for women to interview and contact information for them. Special thanks to Gilbert Savery, David Hamer, Robert Dorr, Mary McGrath, Beverly Pollock, Mary Heng-Braun, Alvin Goodwin, Lynne Grasz, Jan Kreuscher, Janet Pieper, James Clemon, Alfred "Bud" Pagel, Emil Reutzel, Arlo Grafton, Ruth Brown, Carol Zuegner, and the late Keith Blackledge. My apologies to anyone I have omitted from this list.

Beverly Deepe Keever, a distinguished Vietnam War correspondent, began as a source and became a supportive colleague as she labored over her own book on Vietnam for the University of Nebraska Press. Thanks also to Bren Ortega Murphy of Loyola University in Chicago for her many helpful suggestions and for inviting me to present my research there.

I am grateful to my family for its support, especially my mother, Kathleen McGowen Wirth; my brother Mark Wirth and nephew David Wirth; and my children, Raj and Shanti Psota. My close friends Liz Sundem, Jeanne Weeks, Jane O'Brien, and Dianne Travers-Gustafson offered suggestions when they read preliminary versions of chapters and managed to act interested for three years. So did my "Wine & Whine" group, Joyce Bunger, Robyn Eden, and Jan Kruse.

I have enjoyed working with the fine staff of the University of Nebraska Press, especially Heather Lundine, who challenged me to write a book about the first century of women in Nebraska women in journalism, not just the modern era, and Bridget Barry, who guided me in revising and completing this book and patiently responded to all questions. Thanks also to my copy editor, Barbara Wojhoski, for her work in fine-tuning the final text.

FROM SOCIETY PAGE TO FRONT PAGE

Introduction

I can see and hear it as if it were yesterday. The mint-green *Omaha World-Herald* newsroom stretched before me a block long. Cluttered, black-topped army surplus desks equipped with battered manual typewriters filled half of it. Teletype machines clattered rhythmically in the background, while a police dispatch radio broadcast a constant stream of calls that everyone seemed to ignore and the myriad phones rang constantly. Reporters answered promptly, hoping that news sources were responding to their urgent requests for return calls.

Copy editors labored over stories pasted into long scrolls of copy paper, cutting the last few inches off some to fit the space available. They printed their headlines in carbon pencil at the top, noting type size and number of columns. Pneumatic tubes whistled overhead when an editor sent completed copy to the linotype machines in the basement for typesetting. The atmosphere of controlled chaos seemed like something out of *Front Page*.

In a month or so, one of those big black desks would be mine when I joined the news staff after completing my graduate work at the University of Minnesota. Then it hit like a punch in the solar plexus. Where were the women?

At the *Lincoln Evening Journal*, where I had worked on the copy desk the previous summer, there were women reporters and copy editors, even a female assistant city editor. Where were they here? I looked more closely. Guys in white shirts and ties filled the long rows of reporters' desks. Then I saw a woman toward the back of room: Mary McGrath. That seemed to be it for city reporters, although actually there were a few more women in the newsroom, including another reporter, a couple of support staffers, and two night copy editors.

Oh yes! In a distant corner of the room, a group of women were working behind one of the cast-iron fences that divided departments: Women's News or Society, "Sox" in newsroom slang. Probably not everyone was wearing a pastel dress that day, but all I could think of was a flower garden. It speaks volumes that the *World-Herald*'s 1985 centennial history includes a chapter on the sports section but none on women's news. Only a few women's names even appear in the index. What was I getting into?

FAST FORWARD FORTY YEARS

Memories of that first visit flooded back when Business editor Patricia Waters, who has since retired, guided me on a tour of the modern newsroom. I had worked at the *World-Herald* for eleven years before leaving for a public relations job at Union Pacific Railroad in 1980 and finally becoming a journalism professor at Creighton University in 1991. I had not been in the newsroom since the newspaper had moved to a nearby corporate high-rise.

The changes were striking. On my first visit in 1969, I had walked upstairs to the newsroom, unimpeded by security guards. On this visit I had to sign in, get a visitor's badge, and wait for Pat to escort me to the third-floor newsroom. Her employee badge unlocked the door to a newsroom decorated in earth tones instead of institutional green. Gone also were all the clattering machines and the pneumatic tubes. Even the phones seemed muted, or maybe it was just that the upholstered cubicles absorbed their sound. No open rows of army surplus desks for today's reporters!

At first glance the newsroom (which still stretched for a block) might have been an insurance office. Pat halfway apologized, assuming correctly that I preferred the dump of yore because it was part of the romance of journalism. Gone were the hallway observation windows where awed school groups had watched us like animals in the zoo. No one would ever again thrill Cub Scouts by yelling, "Stop the presses!" as an old timer supposedly did one dull day — all in fun, like other newsroom antics.

The major difference I had come to observe also was instantly apparent. Women filled at least a third of the desks in all areas of the room except Sports, where a single longtime staffer was the only female. "Everything but Sports is highly integrated," said Waters, who had joined the paper in 1988 as editor of what is now called Living. Today most of the newsroom middle managers (who head sections or teams of reporters) are women, and assistant managing editor Joanne Stewart rates a private office overlooking the newsroom.

Unlike the old fences that demarcated departmental turf, it's hard to tell where one section starts and another ends. Copy editors no longer sit around a horseshoe shaped "rim" with their boss occupying the "slot" but instead work in cubicles like reporters. Long gone are the scrolls of copy; editors access stories via computer and write headlines the same way, setting the computerized "cold type" with each keystroke. As Waters led me around the newsroom, I saw a few former colleagues who still worked at the paper as well as former students and other friends. Two of my Creighton journalism alums exemplified the difference between the paper then and now.

Lynn Safranek, who has since taken a non-news job in Chicago, had won awards for her coverage of police before joining the Page One team. In the early seventies, editors were nervous about assigning a woman to "cop house." I covered the beat on Saturdays for several years, one of the first Omaha women reporters to do so, although I prayed every Friday that nothing would happen that would increase my chances of making a horrendous error. Some of the younger men who covered police fulltime hated covering the beat as much as I did, but they received valuable training in this entry-level hard-news assignment. No more are women denied this opportunity.

Over in Living (the successor to Women's News), Kevin Coffey covers music and pop culture, his dream job. His cubicle's shelves are filled with CDs. He was listening to one for a review as we strolled by. No more flower gardens in Living! Looking around, no one would guess that a quiet revolution to open this workplace to women was ever required.

Waters, a fellow native of Nebraska City, has worked in newsroom management for most of her career. After graduating from the University of Nebraska College of Journalism in 1975, she joined the *Fremont Tribune*, a Gannett Corporation newspaper. She rose from reporter to managing editor and could have become publisher if she had been willing to live in Fremont. However, by then she was commuting forty miles each way from an Omaha suburb where her husband had become a school principal, so she moved to the *World-Herald*.

In Fremont Waters benefited from Gannett's equal opportunity policies that opened top positions throughout the corporation to talented women. The *World-Herald* lacked such policies, but Waters found an informal mentor in another Nebraska City native, Deanna Sands, the paper's first woman managing editor. After her retirement Sands headed the national Associated Press Managing Editors (APME) group for a period.

Waters typifies another change in journalism from forty years ago. She is a mother who worked in news while raising her two now-grown children, something that would have been almost impossible in 1980, when I left the paper because I wanted a family. The hours were just too long and irregular to balance motherhood and reporting, but today's women journalists are less willing to sacrifice their personal lives for the paper. They can do this because they are thoroughly integrated into the mainstream of journalism, while we were still somewhat on the margins.

Waters salutes the early baby boomers for this change. "They showed the business world that women could do it."

MY STORY

I didn't set out to be a groundbreaker for women in journalism, but as an early baby boomer there was no alternative if I wanted to report on social issues instead of society news. Closed doors begged to be opened; traditional ways of viewing women that made no sense had to be challenged as both a matter of justice and to achieve my goals. Times were good in the early 1970s and jobs plentiful, so my friends and I could take risks, too naive to realize they were risks.

I grew up on a farm near Nebraska City, the second of six bright, strong-willed, competitive children, sandwiched between an older sister who is one of the nation's leading experts on distance education and a younger sister who became the first woman fellow at Bell Labs. My three younger brothers also have had stellar careers, but only later did I realize how extraordinary our family was. My mother, an artist, had been valedictorian of her University of Nebraska class, while my father had a classically trained baritone voice. He had considered a career in music before family duty drove him back to the farm. My parents married during World War II while Mother was in college and they had thought Dad would be drafted. However, when the army decided that it needed farmers more to grow food than to fight, Dad remained in Nebraska City and Mother commuted there from Lincoln on weekends until she graduated. My parents placed a high premium on academic achievement and drove all of us to live up to our potential regardless of sex. Just keeping up in my family was tough, so I took refuge in books, reading everything I could find at the local public library while dreaming of distant places.

I needed to escape because as a short, pudgy, awkward nerd wearing glasses, I became a target for mean girls whose favorite sport was pushing me into trees during junior high. Mother promised that eventually life would get better, but my loathing for people who abuse the weak fueled later newspaper stories and my eagerness to combat unfairness to women. During these miserable years, I decided to become a foreign correspondent because the journalists I read about like my hero, war correspondent Quentin Reynolds, seemed to lead exciting, fun lives. It never occurred to me that Reynolds and his fellow journalists were nearly all men.

I couldn't imagine not having a career, a notion both parents encouraged. As a teenage waitress at Steinhart Lodge, I served numerous luncheons to upper-middle-class women who spent their afternoons playing bridge. The endless card playing seemed like such a waste of talent that I resolved to avoid a similar fate at all costs. In contrast I watched my mother continue to paint and create a remedial reading class at school.

Like all my relatives, I headed to the University of Nebraska for college, the only school I even applied to. Years later an Omaha lawyer asked if I felt deprived because I hadn't gone to an Ivy League school like her children. Excuse me? For us NU was the big time, and we felt lucky to study there because many families didn't "waste" their money educating girls, even at nearby Peru State College. At the university I loved my honors history class so much that I told my parents that I wanted to major in history, not journalism, but my father set me straight. Females who majored in history ended up in the typing pool but a journalism degree could lead to a decent job, so he ordered me to take a journalism course.

NU's journalism school was strong, but my job on our student paper, the *Daily Nebraskan*, turned me into a journalist for life. I adored not only the work but the brilliant, hilarious people who hung out at the paper and yearbook offices. For the first time in my life, I belonged! We lived in almost total sexual equality. Women supervised men as readily as the reverse, and the guys had no use for women who hid their smarts. It was fun to be a student journalist in the mid-1960s because we questioned authority and the outmoded rules that restricted women, and we were optimistic that authorities would see the light and change.

Like many female veterans of student media, I later wanted to re-create the best experience of my life by becoming a full partner on the newsroom team.

After graduating in 1968 with double majors in journalism and political science and minors in history and English, I accepted an assistantship in political science at the University of Minnesota, hoping that a master's degree would help me get a job covering politics or social issues. When I reached the Minnesota campus, I discovered to my surprise that this was the first year that the political science department had not penalized female applicants for their sex. Who would ever have guessed that women had been so unfairly penalized? The faculty had feared that women would drop out of school to get married, wasting a precious opportunity. They were proud of themselves for dropping this sexist restriction, but graduate school gave me my first taste of being a test case for my gender. I did the coursework for the MA and started hunting for a reporting job in Nebraska or Iowa in the spring of 1969.

The timing was good because the economy was booming, and men were being drafted for the Vietnam War. I detested the war, so I did not rejoice in the circumstance even though I benefited from it. Major newspapers were opening city news jobs to women for the first time, and I had my choice of three offers. I took the one at the *World-Herald* because it was closest to home, and I became one of the newspaper's first three or four modern women in city news. Almost immediately I was assigned the church beat, while newly hired men either spent several months on general assignment or the police beat. I was pleased with the assignment because I was interested in religion and saw it as an opportunity to enterprise. It didn't occur to me until later that I had been treated differently than the guys.

As I look back on my eleven years at the paper, my gratitude for what I learned outweighs any complaints about sexism, such as being asked about my possible marriage plans during the interview process. I quickly discarded my inflated notions of my competence. It was painfully obvious how much I had to learn, and having so few women colleagues to commiserate with made this process more difficult. Fortunately Mary McGrath became a combination of mentor and guardian angel, and I owe surviving that first year to her. If a few of the men resented the opening of city news to women, the majority welcomed anyone who was competent and hardworking regardless of sex. Fred Thomas, David Thompson, Jim Clemon, and others went out of their way to be helpful. They along with people like Mary, Bob Dorr, Steve Jordon, and Mike Kelly were a newsroom team that I was proud to be part of. I loved the newsroom's energy and its humor even if some of it would have struck an outsider as dark, off color, or sexist because this humor was our survival mechanism and a badge of belonging.

My religion beat thrust me into covering the social action work in which many religious groups were involved in that era, especially in North Omaha's African American neighborhoods. Covering African American churches entailed writing about their fight for economic empowerment and their protests against racism. At some point local women's groups started speaking out about sex discrimination, and I began routinely covering stories that the guys either did not hear about or did not perceive as newsworthy. Since I was already covering a beat that included many stories about social issues and discrimination, adding women's problems to the list required no special permission. All I had to do was suggest specific stories. The more I wrote about topics such as credit discrimination against women or the lack of a Girls Club comparable to Omaha's outstanding Boys Clubs, the more tips I got and the more my editors welcomed such coverage. As an added bonus, just airing issues could often lead to important changes for women. The stories of Connie Claussen, the University of Nebraska at Omaha's women's athletic director who also taught and coached, and Doris Royal, a farmer from

Sarpy County, illustrate the role that journalism played in correcting blatant injustice based on sex.

Claussen, whom I had met through covering the Mayor's Commission on the Status of Women, called in 1973 to say that she was resigning as women's athletic director at UNO and would merely teach physical education courses. She would no longer coach for free while men were paid. She also complained about teaching in a Quonset hut that lacked showers, while the men's facilities were far nicer. *Great story*, thought I: credible source at a major institution refusing to tolerate discrimination any longer. However, since it was a sports story, I offered it to the UNO beat reporter in Sports. He vehemently rejected the idea, almost yelling that women's sports were not newsworthy. I told the city desk that I wanted to write the piece. After it ran on the front page of the Sunday paper, UNO addressed Claussen's complaints. She built outstanding women's sports programs, and the university replaced the Quonset hut with a new physical education building.

When Doris Royal called, her first question was: "Are you interested in stories about women?" Then she told me something that astounded me despite my farm background. Federal inheritance-tax laws were forcing widows off their farms because the IRS maintained that husbands owned the land and farm earnings. Widows had to pay inheritance taxes that many could not afford on their own homes. Farm wives could escape taxes by demonstrating that they had helped buy the farm through an outside salary or a family inheritance, but farm work didn't count because the IRS did not document it. Royal wanted a story on her petition drive to change this injustice. After I investigated and learned that Royal's facts were correct, I wrote a story that someone passed on to the *Farm Journal*. I learned later that the *Farm Journal* then launched a national petition drive that was instrumental in changing the law. But the law change began with Royal's petition and the coverage that the Omaha media gave it.

At times I crossed the line between objective reporting and advocacy for women, a common problem among female reporters covering women's issues in this era. When the Nebraska legislature held a hearing on repealing our ratification of the proposed Equal Rights Amendment, I took the day off to see my mother testify against repeal. I asked hostile questions of ERA opponent Phyllis Schlafly and struggled to be fair to local anti-ERA forces.

But such hot-button issues were the exception. Mostly I wrote about problems facing women that would otherwise have been overlooked. For example, I covered the struggle to open a spouse abuse shelter that prominent women demanded and many men felt was unnecessary. The executive director of Catholic Charities, which United Way had assigned to run the new program, called me the day after the shelter opened, distraught because he had not believed it was needed yet it filled immediately. By noon of the first day there was a waiting list, and the agency immediately began planning a second facility. The case reminded me that many men simply needed to be educated about the problems of women, and it made me determined to keep writing stories that informed them.

Most of my news sources did not care who covered them as long as the stories were accurate, but most police and many politicians were overtly sexist. The police disliked all reporters, but they especially loved tormenting women like me who substituted on weekends. Crude jokes tested if women would get upset, and many officers made clarifying confusing information on police reports more difficult than necessary just to see if the reporter would get rattled. I'm sure this has changed now that women routinely cover police and many top officers are women. When I finally got a chance to cover politics by assisting Don Pieper at the state legislature, I fielded comments about how kind the newspaper was to send him such an attractive "consort" and so on. I informed one state senator who had complained about being interviewed by the church editor that I had a master's degree in political science from the University of Minnesota; that shut him up. Such comments were a small price to pay for attending Don's ongoing informal seminar in state government, the best graduate education I ever received in this field. Along the way I also learned to avoid wearing miniskirts around politicians who had been drinking.

During my first years at the paper, I felt that everything I did could either help or hurt opportunities for other women because managers still seemed to regard women reporters as an experiment. We had to be as tough as the guys in a tough field and yet remain feminine. Crying was, of course, forbidden as was turning down any assignment, but baking brownies and bantering about baseball won allies. I took foolish risks such as walking to my car alone after covering night assignments to avoid appearing weak. The sensible precaution of asking for an escort after dark did not occur to me, and I would have rejected it if it had. Dumb — and dangerous!

I waged two ongoing battles during those early years because I felt a duty to speak out for women. The first concerned sexism in the news columns and headlines, those casual, cute putdowns of women that weren't meant to offend but did. I retreated readily when my objections were not well received because I didn't want to alienate the guys; mostly they just needed a pleasant reminder that standards had changed. The second dealt with the reluctance of the paper to assign women to hard news beats and to open Sports to them. I didn't want to cover sports, cops, or city hall but felt that women should have the opportunity if they wanted it. After three years I also wanted a new beat because my male peers had all changed assignments at least once during the period. It seemed that there were different policies for women and men. My two causes came together in an incident that endeared assistant city editor Alfred "Bud" Pagel to me forever.

I glanced at the front page of the paper one day when Bud was on the city desk and noticed that the lead on the weather story said that just like a woman, Mother Nature had thrown a fit then stomped out. When I chided Bud for failing to change the sexist language, he told me I was being overly sensitive. I dropped the subject, but the next morning Pagel resumed our conversation. "You know that weather lead you didn't like," he said. "Yes," I replied. "Well maybe you were right. When I got home, the first thing Annie [his wife] said to me was, 'Ew, Bud, how did you let that get in the paper?'" Then instead of heading back to the city desk, Pagel asked, "Do you ever feel you're treated differently because you are a woman?" Was I hearing this correctly? I wondered. "I don't think a man with a master's degree in political science who has worked as hard as I have would be unable to get off the church beat after three years." Bud responded, "You've got a point. Let's talk about it after work tomorrow night."

Over drinks at the Omaha Press Club, Pagel and I discussed women's opportunities compared with those of men of equal ability and experience. Pagel said my work merited a change of assignments, and as we left, he promised, "On Monday you'll have a new beat." On Monday I became the full-time human services reporter covering housing, welfare, nonprofit agencies, services to young and old people, abuse of people by bureaucrats, and other such topics. I have remained forever grateful to Bud and to the other men who helped women become a routine part of our news operation — the primary goal of us groundbreakers. No lawsuit could have done as much for me or for women as a heartfelt talk with a colleague whom I highly esteemed. Thanks, Bud!

Simultaneously the *World-Herald* began hiring more women in city news, including Eve Goodwin, our first African American, and good women journalists were breaking into Omaha TV news. Our hard work paid off as we became increasingly integrated into all aspects of news. The young women (and men) in all forms of Omaha media became friends covering assignments together and socializing at Omaha Press Club events, a cross-media alliance that was especially helpful to women in sorting out common problems. We even did daring things like petition the press club to drop its partnership with another private club that banned women from the dining room; numerous men signed our protest. Together we created a new norm in local news that within a few years made the presence of women in all our newsrooms routine. However, we did it so quietly that even our colleagues did not realize what we had changed and accomplished. By 1977 when the *World-Herald* sent me to Houston to cover the big National Women's Year Conference, the assignment was almost something I had expected even given the rarity of covering anything outside Nebraska. By then my editors realized that the issues being discussed were of great interest to most readers regardless of their views on topics such as the ERA. In fact most members of the Nebraska delegation opposed it, but our readers obviously followed my coverage and I even got the only bonus of my reporting career for my work there.

I left the *World-Herald* for a PR job at Union Pacific Railroad in 1980, the first woman in PR at this predominantly male company. Years later I earned a doctorate in political science (built on that early master's) and became the first female chair of Creighton University's journalism department.

In hindsight I feel fortunate to have come of age when I did and honored to have helped open modern Omaha journalism to women. I could never have enjoyed the career I have had without the support of male as well as female mentors and colleagues, and I am grateful to all of them. For years I thought that we baby boomers were the groundbreaking women in journalism in Nebraska. How wrong I was. As the rest of this book reveals, we were just another link in a chain of remarkable women. I hope that compiling their stories casts new light not only on those in Nebraska journalism but also on the lives of women in many fields throughout the country.

1 | Pioneer Women in Journalism

When Union Pacific Railroad urged Europe's landless masses to move to Nebraska in the late 1860s, it sold a vision of paradise on the prairies. The railroad, headquartered in Omaha, helped create a land boom that raised the state's population from 28,841 in 1860 to 122,993 in 1870. These settlers who found both fertile land and a climate of extremes—heat, cold, blizzards, droughts, tornados to say nothing of occasional insect plague—either learned to cope or left. By 1890 nearly 20 percent of the residents were foreign born, lured by free land or jobs in railroading and meatpacking. The immigrants, especially the Catholics, tended to vote Democratic, while Nebraskans born in the United States were more likely to be Republicans. The immigrants viewed "typical Republican tendencies" to support prohibition and other "coercive cultural measures" as "intolerable efforts . . . to impose Anglo-American Protestant values" on them.

The crash of 1893 hit Nebraska hard with some towns losing population while others stabilized at levels where they remained for decades. The Populist Party, which sought government regulation of rail rates, free silver, and other reforms to help farmers, held its first national convention in Omaha in 1892. Meanwhile, Omaha business leaders responded to the economic crisis by starting the Chamber of Commerce and the Knights of Ak-Sar-Ben and planning the Trans-Mississippi Exposition of 1898. By this period Omaha had become the state's business and financial engine and Lincoln its educational and cultural center. In so many respects the two cities could scarcely have been more different. No matter how many mansions appeared on its "Gold

Coast" in today's midtown area, Omaha remained a hard-working/hard-playing railroad and meatpacking center with a diverse immigrant population as well as the state's only albeit small African American community. Omaha's machine mayor had entered politics to counter a threat to his gambling business, and few Omahans objected to the city's abundance of taverns. Lincoln, the seat of state government, the University of Nebraska, and several other colleges, was far more genteel; there life revolved around discussion clubs, literary societies, the opera house, churches, and the city's thirteen temperance societies.

By 1900 Nebraska's population had stabilized at nearly 1.1 million, with a decreasing percentage of the people living on farms. The number of towns with populations over 2,500 rose from sixteen to twenty-seven, while Omaha and Lincoln also grew. Urban residents boasted of their opera houses and enjoyed amenities such as telephones and running water. In older communities such as Nebraska City and Fremont, elegant brick and frame houses lined the streets, testimony to the "social chasm" between classes that was greater in the 1880s than it had ever been or would be for generations. Author Willa Cather believed that the state benefited from the tests of the 1890s because people who could not endure hardship were "winnowed out" and departed. "The strongest stock survived, and within ten years those who had weathered the storm came into their reward." Thus one of Nebraska's first important women journalists showed that she was a product of her state — a survivor.

The first major influx of women into journalism on a national level coincided roughly with the early days of the Nebraska press. Although a handful of women were involved in journalism before the Declaration of Independence, there were few women journalists until the 1880s, when the industrial age transformed both the nation and the news industry. During this period cities grew rapidly, enrollment in high schools and colleges soared, and the number of periodicals in the nation rose from 4,400 in 1890 to 5,100 in 1895. Men wrote the newspapers of the era for other men, giving their readers a mix of politics, crime news, scandal, and business. Many of these topics were of little interest to over-worked women raising large families and running households in the days before electricity and modern appliances. Since they couldn't vote and had few economic opportunities, why would they spend scarce time on these dense, disorganized pages of gray type with tiny headlines that modern people find almost impossible to read? The lack of women readers meant, however, that advertisers were failing to reach their prime female shop-pers/customers, so they pressured publishers to create a product that would attract more women readers.

In response to such pressure, newspapers created women's so-cial sections focusing on food, fashion, and families and hired women to produce them. Editors also discovered that they could bolster circulation by employing a handful of women as "sob sis-ters" or "stunt girls." The "sob sisters" exploited the pathos in sensational crime and disaster stories, specializing in portrayals of jilted wives, jealous lovers, and devastated children. One of the most famous was Ada Patterson, who lived in Franklin County, Nebraska, from 1877 to 1889 and taught in Lincoln be-fore moving to Salt Lake City to begin her reporting career. She gained national fame for her coverage of sensational murder tri-als in Hearst's *New York Journal* and *Journal-American*. Among other things, she covered several executions, both a hanging in Missouri and an electrocution in New York. A contemporary stated, "Ada Patterson went through the hoops of sensational journalism with the perfect touch for what she was doing. . . . Miss Patterson, under a mild manner, has a shrewd knowledge of human reactions under the light of fierce publicity."

"Stunt girls" were celebrity journalists who gained fame and riveted public attention on their newspapers through a print ver-sion of today's reality TV shows. The most famous of these was Nellie Bly of Joseph Pulitzer's *New York World*, whose highly publicized trip around the world in eighty days included grant-ing a woman reporter from Kearney her only interview en route. There is no evidence that Nebraska papers employed either stunt girls or sob sisters, but they shared the national eagerness to please advertisers by carrying more news of interest to women.

Critics have complained that the sob sisters and stunt girls de-layed the assignment of women to covering hard news. Most women journalists covered mundane news in society sections that were less prestigious and paid less than other newspaper sections. As Anne McCormick, foreign correspondent for the *New York Times*, wrote, they "languish over the society column of the daily newspaper. They give advice to the lovelorn. They edit household departments. Clubs, cooking, and clothes are rec-ognized as subjects particularly fitting to their intelligence." Nonetheless, journalism had become a major employer of pro-fessional women and a way for "respectable women to earn a liv-ing and to voice social concerns." Census data reflect the influx of women into the field. While in 1880 only 288 women worked full-time in journalism out of a national total of about 12,000 journalists, by 1890 there were nearly 2,000 women journalists. The number continued to grow nationally and in Nebraska.

WOMEN PUBLISHERS ENTER NEBRASKA JOURNALISM

The first editor to reach out to Nebraska's women writers was Robert Furnas, founder of the *Nebraska Farmer*. In the maga-zine's first issue in 1859, he wrote, "A number of Nebraska ladies who understand the use of the pen, and are skilled in matters pertaining to the household department, have promised us regu-lar contributions. . . . We hereby, however, extend a general in-vitation to every lady in Nebraska and adjacent thereto, to con-tribute to the columns of the *Farmer.*" Patricia Gaster of the Nebraska State Historical Society, the state's leading expert on women in journalism, was unable to confirm if any women took Furnas up on this offer.

After Furnas's invitation, there are no records of women in journalism until 1867, when Harriet Dakin MacMurphy and her husband, John, began publishing newspapers in various Nebraska towns. During the Victorian era women often shared their husbands' careers, especially in family businesses like small-town newspapers, a practice that continues to the present. Often the women's contributions were hidden, but they were full partners. For example, when the MacMurphys bought the *Blair Times* in 1871, Harriet handled finances and circulation, proofreading and writing. She did the same on the other papers that she and John ran at Plattsmouth, Schuyler, South Omaha, Geneva, and Beatrice. In Beatrice she also wrote the newspaper's social column. Harriet, who outlived her husband by more than thirty years, also served as the *Omaha World-Herald*'s longtime domestic-science editor, and her editorials on food safety helped persuade Congress to pass pure-food laws. Later she became Nebraska's food inspector under four governors and also served as the first permanent secretary of the Nebraska Press Association. In an 1895 article on Nebraska's women journalists that appeared in the *Nebraska Editor, World-Herald* social columnist Elia Peattie described MacMurphy as "a woman of peculiar firmness of mind and loftiness of philosophy" who had "as many staunch friends as any woman in the state." In 2012 MacMurphy was elected to the Nebraska Press Women's Hall of Fame.

Other women who launched their own papers or joined their husbands in family partnerships before larger Nebraska newspapers begin hiring them in the 1880s included Maggie Eberhart, who began publishing the *Platte Valley Independent* in North Platte in 1869, moved her paper to Grand Island in 1870, and married her business partner, Seth Mobley, a year later. Their paper was strongly Republican and instantly successful. On July 9, 1870, it boasted that "no community ever took a greater interest in any paper than the citizens of Grand Island. . . . $940 was subscribed for advertising in one day. . . . $180 was raised in less than six hours." Maggie Mobley was institutionalized for mental problems in the 1890s, and after her release, she wrote and lectured on the poor conditions and ill treatment that she had suffered in the mental institution.

By 1896 there were enough women journalists to form a Women's Auxiliary of the Nebraska Press Association. Such organizations offered support to women who were a minority in their field and among a handful of professional women in their towns. Newspapering was a volatile industry in which papers often came and went rapidly. Many small Nebraska communities had more than one paper because political parties sponsored many of them, but a journalist who offended her political sponsors could lose her business, the fate suffered by Rosa Hudspeth of the *Stuart Ledger*.

When Hudspeth took over the financially ailing northern Nebraska paper in 1901, she assured her readers in an early edition that it was in good hands. "A woman can edit a newspaper without being a freak. Running a newspaper is teaching a public school on a large scale." Hudspeth also insisted that "operating a job press is no harder on a woman than running a washing machine." She was confident because she had grown up in a newspaper family in Newport, Nebraska, and became a publisher after working for a paper in Des Moines, writing two novels, and teaching school. Her six years in Stuart illustrate the difficulties facing small-town publishers, especially if they were single women.

Hudspeth's support of woman's suffrage was controversial, and she found it difficult to socialize with other middle-class women. When an article in the *Ledger* offended members of a women's social club, they expelled her and tried to organize a boycott of the paper. Male editors in neighboring towns made life even harder. According to an article by Gaster, "Some were not satisfied to attribute the lowest motives. They spoke of the lady editor in the most vicious terms. One man said: 'That female amazon who pushes the quill on the *Ledger* is said to be as ugly and ungainly as her writings are vicious and demoralizing. They say she weighs two hundred pounds and looks like the side of a house turned edgewise when she is walking.'" In a speech that she wrote for the 1907 NPA convention (apparently delivered by someone else), Hudspeth discussed the challenges of hiring good printing help and managing the business. She ran into financial problems when she dropped the paper's Republican affiliation and lost the support of local Republicans. This led to her departure from the paper and Stuart in 1907.

Early women publishers sometimes had difficulty being taken seriously in the male-dominated field, especially when they were as young as E. Lena Spear of the *Central City Democrat*. At the age of twenty, when modern aspiring women reporters are still studying journalism in college, Spear was already publishing her own newspaper. A native of Illinois, she lived in several states before taking a job as a typesetter for the *Merrick County Republican*, then moved on to the *Prodigal* at Palmer — all before finishing high school. A week after graduation she became publisher of the *Central City Democrat*, which despite its name she proclaimed to be the "paper of no organ or class."

When Spear was invited to address the Nebraska Press Association in 1902, she described the experience of being a young female publisher. "At home I have often had the experience of having a stranger enter the office, take no notice of me at the desk, but look around until he found a boy or a tramp printer reading the exchanges and inquire of this representative of the male persuasion if he were the editor." In response to her complaint that female editors didn't receive treats from news sources such as cigars, her fellow editors presented her with a box of chocolate creams.

Peattie's 1895 article on Nebraska's early women journalists, reprinted in a 1923 history of the Nebraska press, demonstrates that women were active in the field in small towns throughout the state and also published specialized papers aimed at women. She documented the following women as active in publishing at the time: Harriet Dakin MacMurphy, *Beatrice Times*; Edith M. Pray, *Geneva Gazette*; E. Lena Spear, *Central City Democrat*; Anna L. Dowden, *North Bend Republican*; Mrs. E. M. Correll, *Hebron Journal*; Libbie L. Fitch, *Tekamah Weekly Burtonian*; Mary Fairbrother, *Omaha Women's Weekly*; Sarah Butler Harris, *Lincoln Courier*. A later historian for the Nebraska Press Association expanded Peattie's list to include Mary Hitchcock, *Mutual Insurance Journal* (Lincoln); Annie Vio Gates, *Blair Tribune*; Eunice Haskins, *Stella Press*; Chattie Coleman (Mrs. J. A. Westenius), *Stromsburg Headlight*; Mary (Pershing) Butler, *Nebraska Legal News* (Lincoln).

THE GROWTH OF SOCIAL NEWS

As Nebraska grew more urban, social news became more important. On major holidays like New Year's Day, for example, papers published "lists of who would be entertaining so friends could stop by" in compliance with elaborate Victorian social conventions. Like some other papers, the *Omaha Evening World-Herald* offered a woman's column before it developed a women's section. Peattie's "A Word with the Women" became so well known in the 1890s that headlines of her articles, columns, and editorials sometimes featured her name, as these examples illustrate: "The Vital Thing Debt: Mrs. Peattie Discourses on It in Connection with Mortgage Statistics" or "Salvation Lasses at Home: Mrs. Peattie Writes of the Blue Frocked Sisterhood of the Lord."

Social news of the era rarely carried bylines, but it is safe to assume that by the 1890s women whose names have been lost to history wrote the social items in most papers, especially the larger papers in Lincoln and Omaha. One early Lincoln society reporter, Annie L. Miller, later recounted the challenges of the job that she had performed for the *Nebraska State Journal* beginning in 1898. Miller recalled that male colleagues had a low opinion of her function. Her city editor "saw that [she] always had the uninteresting minor assignments that always fall to the greenest reporter." However, Miller said that social reporters found their work anything but tame. "In the eyes of the other reporters my pages were made up chiefly from trivialities, but I easily learned that the perusal of the affairs of nations could cause no such heart-burnings as arose through the society columns. A gentleman of intelligence and culture has been known to appear as chagrined as a defeated politician because of the omission of his wife's name from the report of an important function, and the leaving out of a name of an assisting lady at a reception has more than once aroused the suspicion that the hostess had taken this method of stabbing a friend in the back." In addition to coping with such stresses, social reporters worked grueling hours. "I have arisen from sleep at 7 o'clock in the morning to answer the telephone and hear objections to a musical criticism, and have responded to the bell at midnight to take down a club notice which a lady feared to leave til morning lest she should forget."

NEBRASKA WOMAN SCOOPS THE NATION

Occasionally a Nebraska woman journalist escaped the mundane tasks that Miller describes, none more spectacularly than Maud Marston of Kearney, who intercepted *New York World* "stunt girl" Nellie Bly on her 1889 trip around the world to test if she could complete it in the eighty days made famous by Jules Verne's novel. As the nation became fixated on the stunt (the era's equivalent of a reality TV hit), reporters all over the country fought to interview Bly as she sped through their areas, but Marston of the *Kearney Enterprise* was the only one who succeeded. Her paper persuaded the *World*'s publisher, Joseph Pulitzer, to allow Marston to ride through western Nebraska with Bly. But things became complicated when a January snowstorm closed the railroad tracks and Bly was rerouted through Kansas City. Marston discovered the change and caught up with Bly there even as a *Chi-*

cago Tribune reporter who had hoped to catch Bly in Omaha was left stranded by the route change. During the ride to Galesburg, Illinois, Bly told Marston about her career and the trip, including her interview with Verne, who doubted she could make the trip in seventy-five days (she actually completed it in seventy-two days). Marston wrote her story in Galesburg, then wired it to the *Enterprise* for the next morning's paper, winning high praise from newspapers around the Midwest and also from Bly, who said: "During the early night I had the companionship of Miss Maud Marston of the *Kearney (Neb.) Enterprise*, who came 600 miles to interview me. . . . Miss Marston has been writing under the nom de plume of Miss Muffett, her pet name at home. She has grit and good sense and will succeed."

It is interesting to note that Bly, the nation's most famous woman journalist, later traveled to the Valentine area to investigate the plight of drought-stricken farmers who had lost their entire 1894 corn crop and discovered that reports of the disaster were accurate. "One glimpse of the home life out from the railroads and one is convinced that the tales of destitution in Nebraska have not been exaggerated. I drove over thirty miles around the country (near Valentine) to-day and I saw nothing but misery and desolation." Bly's series of articles is credited with encouraging eastern relief efforts for the Midwest.

NEWSPAPER DEPICTIONS OF NEBRASKA WOMEN IN 1888

In the newspapers of 1888, very little space was devoted to women, and male editors and reporters stereotyped women even when they wrote stories about them to attract female readers. Every issue of the *Evening World-Herald* during the weeks of January 8 and January 15, 1888, contained at least one such major article. All used flowery language to pay deference to respected women but which seemed to deny their individuality and full humanity (warts and all).

For example, a story in the January 14, 1888, paper profiled

Elizabeth Reeves, eighty-nine, "Omaha's Oldest Settler." The semi-reverent language that describes "ladies" fails to reflect the difficulties of life in early Omaha or Reeves's feelings about her life. This is a story about a woman as an object, not as a subject reflecting on her experiences. "For thirty years she has been a guardian angel in Omaha gliding here and there and with her sweet smile and cheerful words lifting the clouds from many a home and making many a heart leap with gladness that was unknown before. Scarcely a week but she may be seen seeking the bedside of the sick and dying—bringing in her very presence all that the weary could need." Where is the gritty realism of Willa Cather's Nebraska women coping imperfectly with the hardships of frontier life? What do such profiles say about how women were stereotyped in the eyes of male journalists and the popular imagination?

Two other articles that seem particularly revealing were both in the January 21 issue. Both speak volumes about the roles and presumed concerns of the upper-class women whom the paper was obviously trying to reach. One described the benefits of educating young women, even those whose families employed "hired girls," to cook and perform other household tasks. The other advised readers about the intricacies of making proper social introductions. Although this article discouraged introducing "ladies of the same city to each other" and making introductions in drawing rooms, exceptions were permissible. "Many well poised hostesses have, however, taken liberty with the law of no introductions in their drawing rooms. They are sufficiently women of the world to know that any other woman of the world can shun the odious Mrs. Von Stoffenburg if she chooses and if she prefers to help make the shy, the stranger within her gates, comfortable." The first reminds us of the social and economic class distinctions among women of the era, even in a prairie state that had recently been frontier. How many Omaha families could afford "hired girls" compared with families where young women had to hire out to such families? How many girls of the era received much education at all, and how many were forced to quit school to earn income or to help care for their families, as both of my grandmothers were?

The article on proper social introductions seems especially pretentious, even silly, but probably pleased advertisers from high-end Omaha stores trying to reach their potential customers. Certainly the issue was nothing that Willa Cather's women would have had time to worry about, let alone the immigrant women crowding South Omaha's packinghouse neighborhoods or African American women in North Omaha. But it must have been the talk of morning tea in the mansions on the Gold Coast, possibly inspired by a conversation that an editor had with his wife. I assume that stories in the 1880s were assigned on this basis because they certainly were in the 1970s, when editors would occasionally cite such kitchen-table discussions as the source of a news tip. It's fun to envision women in social news rolling their eyes at such assignments just as their modern descendants did. Catering to the interests of the few is a consistent pattern in Omaha social news during many decades. Such coverage often contrasts sharply with the headlines in the rest of the newspaper and the lives of women readers.

A FINAL WORD FROM A FOREMOTHER

Despite the difficulties they faced, by the turn of the last century women had earned a niche, albeit a usually limited one, in Nebraska journalism. Peattie's 1895 article celebrating the accomplishments of her female colleagues stated: "The woman reporter and correspondent has become an accepted factor in metropolitan newspaper work. Everyone is aware of her existence, realizes that she has a place to fill, knows she is paid as well as the men who work with her, and almost everyone reads her 'stuff.'"

Well, yes and no. Peattie herself was the closest thing Nebraska had to a celebrity woman journalist and this might have colored

her assessment. She might have been paid as well as the men because of her fame but that would have been atypical. She also had
seen a great deal of progress during her years in the state, much
as we did in the early 1970s. Knowing that using pleasant fictions
can help achieve goals, I suspect she was deliberately playing to
an audience of male journalists, encouraging them to recognize
women as part of their newsroom teams. So yes, by the end of
this era, women had become part of Nebraska journalism to stay,
and yes, people read their work. However, it might be wise to
view the remainder of the quote as an effort to promote the full
acceptance of women in the field rather than as a statement of
fact.

2 | Three Superstar Journalists

Three of the most important women journalists in Nebraska history were contemporaries in the first decades in which women worked in the field, and they deserve a chapter devoted to their groundbreaking work. Although Willa Cather remains a household name, many identify her only with her novels, and her journalistic career is often overlooked. Elia W. Peattie and suffragist editor Clara Bewick Colby have largely been forgotten. This is regrettable because both made important contributions. As stated in the previous chapter, Peattie's column was the forerunner of the *World-Herald*'s women's news/Living section, but she is not even mentioned in the *World-Herald*'s centennial history, which includes a chapter on the sports section but none on the women's section. Colby published the nation's second longest running suffragist paper.

When Peattie, who had been a "girl reporter" and society editor in Chicago, moved to Omaha with her newspaper editor husband Robert in 1888, rich women spent their days trading social calls in their ornate homes and debating the fine points of Victorian etiquette. But she was too busy for social calls as she delved into every corner of Omaha life for her "A Word with the Women" column in the *Evening World-Herald*. She became a local celebrity through a column that mixed reporting, social commentary, and announcements of upcoming events. She was also the first to publicize Cather's talent, stating in an 1895 article, "If there is a woman in Nebraska newspaper work who is destined to win a reputation for herself, that woman is Willa Cather."

Cather launched her writing career by reviewing dramas for the *Nebraska State Journal* and the *Lincoln Courier* during her student days at the University of Nebraska. Later she took journalism jobs outside the state while pursuing her passion for writing novels that immortalized the experience of Nebraska pioneer women. In Beatrice, Nebraska, women found yet another journalist who gave voice to their aspirations. Clara Bewick Colby published the *Woman's Tribune*, a weekly suffragist newspaper that became an important voice of the national movement in the 1880s and 1890s. It is little short of astonishing that three such remarkable women worked simultaneously in a state with fewer than a million people and that their writings reveal so much about life in the era. It is also fascinating that Peattie and Colby are not usually mentioned in the histories of Nebraska, although Cather is such an icon that no historian can overlook her or avoid quoting her views on Nebraska.

ELIA PEATTIE'S OMAHA

To read a collection of Peattie's columns from her eight years in Omaha is to vicariously experience life in the Victorian-era city, a wealthy community emerging from its rough frontier origins to become a regional metropolis. Peattie's primary focus was always the lives of women, but some columns reveal her concern for other underdogs such as the local African American community. One might well view her as one of the first modern women: a consummate multitasker who also lectured and wrote novels, short stories, and even a railroad travel guide to support her family. Peattie, who gave birth to the third of her four children in Omaha, had no choice but to earn additional money to support her growing family after Robert fell seriously ill and never fully recovered.

An ardent suffragist, Peattie ran unsuccessfully for a seat on the Omaha school board, the only office for which women could vote, and she helped the national Woman's Club movement take root in Nebraska. These clubs became significant vehicles for upper-class women to promote social causes such as public libraries and child welfare. After Robert lost his job in Omaha due to his illness, the Peattie family returned to Chicago. However, Elia Peattie left behind a mosaic of writing about life in a city where she came of age professionally. Susanne George Bloomfield has compiled this work into a book called *Impertinences*, which introduces modern readers to this remarkable woman. In 2007 Peattie was elected to the Nebraska Press Association Hall of Fame, two years after Bloomfield's book finally called attention to her achievements.

Peattie visited areas of Omaha unknown to most women of her social class such as South Omaha's slaughterhouses. I picture her traveling to her assignments on a streetcar in full Victorian attire regardless of what she was covering because she didn't have the option of donning a pair of jeans to do a dirty job like women reporters today. I try to imagine the scene at the Cudahy plant (where nearly two thousand people worked) when Peattie arrived to describe the process of killing cattle for her February 7, 1892, column. "The work is unrelenting from the time the whistle blows in the morning, till the night. The young Bohemian who stands with his legs well apart, and his fine arms half bared at the end of a chute where cattle run from the brown hillside, never alters from the steady down-falling of his big hammer. And each fall of that hammer knocks into insensibility a beef."

Peattie's columns cover an astonishing range of subjects. One day we see her visiting a slaughterhouse and the next satirizing the pretentiousness of Omaha's upper-class women, whom she accused of undermining Omaha's prosperity by shopping for luxury goods elsewhere. In a February 8, 1891, column she noted, "There is nothing that cannot be obtained here," and cited the quality of Omaha's retail offerings. "There are houses that import unique dress patterns from Paris, every sort of lace can be procured here, every kind of underclothing, the very latest things in wraps. Why," she asked, "do women send east and go east to buy their household supplies? Why do they wait till they are on their way to the seaside to purchase their summering dresses at Philadelphia and Boston? Can they not recognize fine goods? If they can, they will buy in Omaha, for they can find shops here at which they can buy anything — if they only understand the art of shopping."

Peattie may have enjoyed tweaking the rich, but she had a deep affinity for women and girls who struggled and greatly admired those who served others such as teachers, social workers, Salvation Army members, and nuns. An example of this emerges in her November 1, 1891, column, which painted a vivid picture of nursing sisters at Saint Joseph Hospital.

> The Sister who opened the door to me wore the black swathings that showed her to be under perpetual vows. She led me from room to room; here I saw a Sister holding the head of a woman hideous with the last emaciation of consumption, her breath coming in rattling reluctance, her lips burned with fever, her eyes starting, yet seeing nothing. Back and forth over that distrait head, went the slow hand of the patient Sister. With a never failing smile, the water was lifted and put between those lips, paralyzed with pain. In another room I saw a little boy in the first shock that followed the amputation of his limbs and beside him sat a Sister with her hand on his pulse her whole being alive to his necessity, her skill required to its utmost. . . . Heavens! How far away it seemed from the fret and the fume and the littleness of the rest of us women! To say that I felt secular is putting it mildly. I felt actually profane, and was relieved when I got out among people just as frivolous, as selfish and heedless as I was myself.

Peattie battled for better pay and working conditions for working women and day care for their children by writing vignettes that showed how difficult life was for them and that revealed how they cared for one another. For example, in her August 21, 1892, column, she commented,

> I've often noticed the girls in dry goods stores. They are a good illustration of the point I wish to illustrate. There they stand, tired, dusty, harassed by senseless customers, the day stretching out before them in interminable length, yet almost always they are kind to each other, and are sisterly and courteous. There are exceptions. But the exceptions are few. On streetcars women are almost always particularly nice to each other. In the offices down town they seem to be generally kind and polite. And in society there is not half the idle gossip and ill-nature that there is commonly supposed to be.

Peattie's columns often offered readers a memorable slice of life as she did in her July 19, 1891, column describing riding the streetcar around the city.

> There was the young man with the compelling perfume who carried a roll of music and whose barber had put oil on his hair. . . . There was the kindergarten teacher with her sweet face . . . and the man with the look of a London missionary who gave a tract and punched nickel to the conductor. . . .
> And there was a man in blue jeans who sat with a little child in his arms. . . . And every now and then he drew the little one closer to him, half baring his arm as he did so. And though it was not very hot there were great drops of sweat on that arm, showing through the dirt and tan. And there were other drops on the man's brow. But the child did not notice them and fell asleep in his arms, holding one brawny thumb in its little fist. And then a drop fell on its face right where the last swept over the cheek. But the drop did not come from the brow of the man or yet from the arm.

In her September 25, 1892, column Peattie offered readers a respectful portrait of Omaha's African American community of about six thousand people.

> If it was the intention of the white man to break the spirit of
> the black man then he has failed. . . . The children are in the
> public schools. The women are almost all in their homes,
> comparatively few of them being at any sort of work which
> takes them away from homes. The employments of the men
> are many. But they would have been yet more varied if it had
> not been that the doors of opportunity have so often been
> closed to the man with colored blood in his veins. Certain
> occupations have thus far been closed to such. It is doubtful
> for example, if a colored merchant would succeed. There are
> none in Omaha.

Unfortunately Omaha's African Americans continued to live in
segregated neighborhoods, were banned from numerous jobs,
and seldom appeared in the local newspapers except in crime or
sports stories until the modern civil rights movement began to
force changes.

These samples of Peattie's work not only reveal a great deal
about her and Omaha but position her as a forerunner of women
writers today who have their own blogs and attract numerous
followers on Twitter. She is a woman who deserves to have many
"followers" (in Twitter parlance) because of all she did and the
value of the work she left behind.

WILLA CATHER'S ROOTS IN NEBRASKA JOURNALISM

Although Cather is a giant of literature for her novels, she laid
the roots for that success in her first career, including her first
brief years as a journalist in Nebraska. Cather came of age when
the literary world was torn between realism and sentimentalism,
and she experimented with both styles as a student at the University of Nebraska. The decisions she made in school and as a
novice reviewer at the *Nebraska State Journal* shaped her writing
future. As a novelist Cather crafted powerful, concrete images of
Nebraska's prairies, but long before then she had told her staff

on the university's student literary magazine the *Hesperian* to write in "plain" and "unornamented" language.

Although Cather had published high school news in the *Webster County Argus* at Red Cloud, she originally planned to study medicine at the University of Nebraska but changed her career goal to writing after a professor published one of her literary themes in the *Nebraska State Journal*. She studied journalism under Will Owens Jones, who also was managing editor of the *Nebraska State Journal* and in 1893 hired her to write drama reviews and columns for the paper. During the next nine years, Cather wrote between five hundred and six hundred reviews and columns in addition to publishing poetry, short stories, and plays in the *Hesperian*. A typical day found her heading to one of Lincoln's two theaters to cover a performance after finishing classes. Afterward she went to the newspaper office to write her review by hand since typewriters were a recent, expensive invention, and apparently there were not enough to go around. Finally a copyboy would escort her home.

Cather was determined to have a career, but unlike Peattie she had no use for women's clubs. She distanced herself from women who did not work outside their homes. She feared that domesticity would undermine her ambitions, and as a single woman she supported herself as a journalist for twenty years. She continued writing part time for the *Nebraska State Journal* following her graduation from NU in 1895 and also was a contributor and editor at the *Lincoln Courier* before leaving Lincoln in 1896 for a journalism job in Pittsburgh. She eventually moved to New York to work as an editor at *McClure's* magazine, an important muckraking publication.

When she finally turned to writing novels full-time, Cather drew her inspiration from her roots and her clean, concrete style from her years in journalism. "I had searched for books telling about the beauty of the country I loved, its romance, the heroism, the strength and courage of its people that had been plowed into the very furrows of its soil and I did not find them. So I wrote *O Pioneers.*" Other powerful novels followed, most notably *My Ántonia*, arguably her greatest work.

I fell in love with Cather's work in high school after my mother ordered me to read *My Ántonia*. Although NU's J-School bragged about Cather being an alum, until I undertook this project, I had no idea how lengthy and distinguished her journalistic career had been or how strongly her work in journalism had influenced the writing style of her novels. I envision her as a forerunner of journalists today like Pulitzer Prize–winner Carl Hiaasen who turn to fiction to tell true stories that the strict rules of newswriting will not allow; they nonetheless remain journalists at heart, and their writing styles retain a strong journalistic flavor. Ironically Cather's career suggests that if journalists want more than fleeting fame, they should write fiction that continues to be read for decades rather than newspaper articles that vanish within days.

CLARA BEWICK COLBY: NEBRASKA'S SUFFRAGIST EDITOR

A suffragist newspaper in Beatrice, Nebraska, during the 1880s? Really? How unexpected, cool, but bizarre, thought I when I stumbled across this fascinating information while doing research at the Nebraska State Historical Society during college. It's the kind of oddity that a journalist tends to remember and track down someday. This project became "someday" as I finally learned the story of Clara Bewick Colby and her groundbreaking newspaper, which is one of the major historical sources of information about the national suffrage movement. Colby, a native of England, was a lifelong rebel and an outspoken advocate of women's rights long before she started the *Woman's Tribune*. She moved to Wisconsin as a child and graduated from the university as valedictorian after taking courses previously reserved for men. She left her first job as an instructor there, protesting unequal pay. After marrying her attorney husband, Leonard, she moved to Beatrice, Nebraska, in 1872 and adopted a son, Clarence, from an orphan train. Her involvement in the suffrage movement expanded after she brought Elizabeth Cady Stanton and Susan B. Anthony to lecture in Beatrice in 1878, and she began lecturing nationally for suffrage as one of Stanton's "girls" or "lieutenants."

Colby found her life's mission when she started the *Woman's Tribune* as the monthly newspaper of the Nebraska Woman Suffrage Association in 1883. In 1887 the *Woman's Tribune* became a weekly newspaper and also the official voice of the Kansas Equal Suffrage Society. Nebraska's scattered suffrage proponents needed a specialized newspaper because the state's daily papers provided limited coverage of their issue, and local papers hardly mentioned the association's annual gatherings. Colby's paper provided isolated women with comprehensive coverage of major suffragist meetings, state and national legislative developments, and movement speeches. It also carried international news about women. Where else could one find a multipart series on the condition of women in Egypt? The *Woman's Tribune* took a broad view of suffrage as encompassing more than women getting the vote. While that was the paper's major focus, it also carried stories on women's legal rights, economic empowerment, household hints, health, religion, and childrearing because Colby was concerned about all aspects of women's lives. A single issue might contain the full text of a Susan B. Anthony speech, instructions for building a fire out of corncobs, and a Nebraska suffragist's wedding announcement.

The newspaper turned Colby, the longtime president of the Women's State Association of Suffrage in Nebraska, into a national leader. From 1886 to 1889 the *Woman's Tribune* was the official publication of the National Woman Suffrage Association.

Colby continued publishing the *Woman's Tribune* until 1909, moving it first to Washington DC in 1889, when her husband became assistant attorney general there, and then to Portland, Oregon, in 1904. She divorced Leonard in 1906 because of his infidelity and died in 1916, four years before women won full suffrage and a year before Nebraska gave women the right to vote for president. Her accomplishments include publishing the *Woman's Tribune* for twenty-six years, second longest of any movement paper and longest of any paper without national support, providing her readership base with a national perspective and attracting readers, including men, who would not otherwise have read a suffrage newspaper. The paper became an archival record of the movement through its publication of speeches, events, and figures unrepresented elsewhere.

Merely listing Colby's accomplishments fails to convey the vitality of her journalism. If she were a contemporary writer, she would probably be running an interactive website where readers could share the details of their lives that mainstream media overlook. Because Colby saw suffrage and the economic and legal empowerment of women as inexorably linked, her paper constantly suggested novel ways for women to expand their income. For example, several 1884 articles encouraged women to cultivate silkworms or take up beekeeping. A proponent of beekeeping stated, "I am satisfied that as a specialty it is not so laborious as washing day and, while it is a fact that a whole week may demand hard, uninterrupted labor, I have yet to see one who did not get through it quite as well as with house cleaning or harvesting." Colby's major concerns also included educating women about their legal rights, and most issues contained articles about women and the law. Property rights were a primary concern; in one issue Colby informed readers that under Nebraska state law, for example, women retained the right to control the property that they brought into a marriage, a key issue for farm women who had inherited land. The newspaper told readers that the law stated, "She [a married woman] may sell, give away or mortgage it; and she may devise and dispose of it through her last will and testament in writing the same as though unmarried."

Colby understood that the daily lives of women revolved around mundane matters such as keeping house and raising families, so her paper carried "household hints" such as the aforementioned instructions for making a fire from corncobs: "Take a few cobs and with a hatchet cut them into two inch pieces. Put them into a can and cover them with kerosene oil, have little sheet iron tongs made to handle the cobs with, on the plan of the old sugar tongs. One piece is sufficient to build a fire with a small handful of kindling. Put the cob in the grate and the pieces of kindling around it. It is a success and so little work." Colby also took a great interest in health issues such as the restrictions that female fashions imposed on wearers. In a typical health note, a male doctor offered his thoughts on the harm such costumes did to women. "If we should see a strong draught horse, harnessed with the pressure on the loins, we would pity him; but delicate woman is ignorantly obliged to carry her heavy clothing around her loins without pity for herself."

Women old enough to remember the ridicule feminists endured in the 1970s can appreciate the support that the *Woman's Tribune* offered to isolated suffrage proponents such as Clara A. Young, who lived "in Custer County, Neb., on a ranch twenty miles from town and forty from a railroad station." The paper noted that Mrs. Young wrote columns for the *Republican*, a paper published in Broken Bow, and she represented Nebraska at a national suffrage conference in Minneapolis. Colby also frequently saluted the accomplishments of women leaders such as two women in Arnold, Nebraska. "The *Bugle Call*, edited and published at Arnold, Nebraska by Anna M. Saunders has changed from a quarterly to a monthly. . . . As Arnold is a 'Women's Rights' town, the *Call* says, the postmaster is a woman, Mrs. Harding." A few women surprisingly even got involved with the military. For example, the paper reported that "Firth, Nebraska has an artillery battery composed of ladies. The battery took part at the recent celebration at Wymore and did good work with their field piece, adding to the interest of the occasion." This activity might still be unusual enough to rate coverage.

Despite the diversity of information that the *Woman's Tribune* provided, its focus remained on suffrage and the allied temperance movement. It celebrated accomplishments such as the ability of Nebraska women property owners with school-age children to vote in school elections. In 1887 it collected female voting statistics in several local school elections. "Fifteen women voted at Wilber. At Blair, 236 ballots were cast. At school district 67, Gage County, six women voted and two were nominated for director but declined to serve. In Oakdale forty women voted." A final sample item from Falls City, Nebraska, epitomizes the quirky content of the paper and its interest in everything that women did, some of which strikes a modern reader as hilarious. I particularly loved this report on women who performed a harmonica concert for temperance because I can envision the prim members of my great-grandmother's generation attending it and sipping tea or lemonade afterward. "Our harmonica quartette — Miss Hattie Crow and the Misses Newkirk — who so acceptably rendered prohibition songs at Beatrice, Lincoln and scores of other places in the State, were lately invited by our leading citizens to give a concert here."

While Colby was more of an advocate than traditional journalists such as Peattie and Cather, she seems to deserve a place of honor in the annals of Nebraska journalism because of the groundbreaking nature of her work and the national importance of her paper as a record of the suffrage movement. Eventually she should join Peattie and Cather in the Nebraska Press Association Hall of Fame.

REFLECTION ON THE GIANTS

Both Peattie and Colby illustrate the importance of recognizing the contributions of women working in regional journalism rather than just the Nellie Blys of the era, who became famous because they wrote from New York. American journalism has always been more than just the sum of the New York papers, but too often little attention is paid to significant regional figures and publications, although, as noted in the introduction, I suspect that this situation is slowly changing. Peattie's columns and Colby's paper are potential gold mines for social historians studying how middle-American women lived during the Victorian era, and both are role models for women who still struggle to balance careers and families, activism and domesticity. Peattie is more conventional in this respect, but Colby's struggles with a difficult and unfaithful husband must surely resonate with today's women, who no longer expect their heroines to be spared such difficulties. The work of Peattie and Colby illustrates the truth in the cliché that journalism is the first draft of history but unfortunately history that has too often overlooked both women and the nation outside the major cities of the East Coast.

Cather is such a major literary figure that her journalistic roots tend to be slighted although she spent about twenty years in the field. Her career illustrates the relationship between great journalism and great literature, and her novels shaped many of the long-standing images of women pioneers. Exploring her roots in journalism deepens our understanding of Nebraska's most important author.

Collectively these three giants of journalism have left a rich legacy that contributes greatly to our understanding of women in the heartland in this period and how they responded to the challenges of being bright, talented women writers at a time when this was only marginally acceptable in society. One richly deserves her lasting acclaim, and I hope this book introduces the other two to modern readers.

3 | The Progressive Era

The Progressive Era at the turn of the century was anything but progressive for women despite their continuing involvement in the suffrage and temperance movements and some organized efforts to improve conditions for working women. Men ran business and politics, even, as a Time-Life book on the period notes, "dispensing justice and wisdom to their families like Oriental potentates." In some states restaurants and hotels could refuse to serve unescorted women, and in 1904 New York City jailed a woman for smoking a cigarette in public. Despite a few noted female muckrakers like Ida Tarbell, most women journalists toiled anonymously in newspaper society sections even as politicians like President Theodore Roosevelt busted trusts and protected the public with pure food and drug laws for which women journalists like Harriet Dakin MacMurphy of Omaha had fought. The nation also was being reshaped by a massive influx of immigrants, who fueled its population growth. In Nebraska Progressives scored notable victories that reshaped the state when they regulated railroads and breweries and restricted child labor. However, local women journalists were confined to social reporting instead of covering such issues. Omaha-born Rheta Childe Dorr, who used her New York society column to crusade for immigrant slum women, suffrage, and other causes, was a notable exception to the era's marginalization of women journalists.

Meanwhile, the battle over woman's suffrage continued in Nebraska and nationally until 1920, when the nation ratified the Nineteenth Amendment to the U.S. Constitution. Nebraska's road to ratification and suffrage was rocky to the end; Omaha business leaders, the German-American Alliance, and the brewing industry opposed several initiative and referendum petitions because of the linkage of the suffrage and temperance causes. However, with the coming of World War I, anti-German sentiment boosted support for suffrage. In 1917 the Nebraska legislature allowed women to vote in local elections, but suffrage opponents mounted another referendum campaign that suffrage forces successfully challenged in court. National events finally overtook the state battle when Congress passed the Nineteenth Amendment and the Nebraska legislature ratified it unanimously.

Only one woman journalist with Nebraska roots stands out in the Progressive Era, but Rheta Childe Dorr is such a larger-than-life figure that her color and outrageousness help compensate for the lack of standout women in this period. Most women journalists in this period worked in society sections without the bylines or celebrity promotion that had made Elia Peattie a personality. But Dorr demonstrates that Progressive Party orator and presidential candidate Williams Jennings Bryan was not the only oversized personality from Nebraska to make a major national impact during these years.

Dorr was born in Omaha in 1866, the daughter of a doctor who had stayed in Nebraska after Civil War army service fighting Indians. From the start Rheta could not tolerate the notion that women were inferior to men. As a child, if she heard someone ask whether a neighbor was disappointed by the birth of a daughter instead of a son, she would jump up and down and holler: "Lil girls just as good as lil boys! Lil girls just as good as lil boys!" It was an omen of things to come. At age twelve she sneaked out of her parents' house to attend a women's rights rally led by Elizabeth Cady Stanton and Susan B. Anthony; her parents discovered what she had done when a newspaper printed the names of those who had joined the National Woman Suffrage Association. She spent an unhappy year at the University of Nebraska in 1884–85, living at home with her parents (who had apparently moved to Lincoln) and feeling misunderstood at both school and home. "My professors were as intolerant of me as were my parents, and it seemed to me that I had no friends at all except books." However, her life changed the day a literature professor gave her a copy of Henrik Ibsen's *A Doll's House*; the plight of Nora, a wealthy woman who rebelled against her controlling husband, crystallized Dorr's anger about her sheltered life, and like Nora, she rebelled. To her family's dismay, the day after she finished reading the play she found a job clerking at the post office. There she was exposed to immigrants from Russia, Bohemia, Bulgaria, Germany, Italy, Transylvania, Turkey, and other countries; the experience opened her eyes to lives very different from hers and planted seeds of empathy for underdogs. This empathy motivated her journalistic crusades for the oppressed for years to come. "The life of the town flowed through the post-office corridors. . . . I came to know farmers and ranchers, especially the new settlers from world's ends of which school geographies made no mention. . . . I learned that the world was wide . . . and that from whatever remote hinterland they came, people were people. . . . My social instincts were born in the post-office, my lifelong international sympathies." Dorr struggled to find a career, thinking first of acting because she loved theater and "wanted to play Nora." She tried unsuccessfully to persuade the local opera house to present *A Doll's House* and dreamed of a future elsewhere. "Somewhere far away from my present environment there must be others like Nora, like myself! I looked over my bank account, the savings of two years' work in the post-office, and resolved to go forth in search of my kind."

Dorr left for art school in New York in 1890 and paid only brief visits to Nebraska afterward, but she remained a rebel. In 1892 she married John Pixely Dorr of Seattle and had a son, Julian Childe. After divorcing John because he opposed her need for independence, she moved back to New York, where she found a job as society editor of the *New York Post* in 1892 and struggled to support her son. In her society columns she spotlighted the terrible working conditions of slum women and crusaded for their right to unionize. Her 1910 book, *What Eight Million Women Want*, told the story to a national audience and detailed Dorr's success in persuading the influential Federation of Women's Clubs to back improved conditions for working women.

Always a militant suffragist, in 1914 Dorr led five hundred members of the General Federation of Women's Clubs in presenting President Woodrow Wilson with a suffrage resolution. She also confronted Wilson about his support for letting states decide the issue. "If that is the case, Mr. President," she asked, "would you kindly tell us why you actively approved the amendment to the Constitution providing for direct election of the United States Senators?" "I think it is not proper for me to stand here and be cross-examined by you," Wilson responded.

Ever restless, Dorr persuaded her new employer, the *New York Mail*, to send her to Russia to cover the revolution that had broken out after the czar's abdication in 1917. She wrote dramatically about a unit of female soldiers, although at least one modern historian has criticized Dorr for writing her stories about the "battalion of death" after leaving Russia rather than on deadline as male war correspondents did. Nonetheless, she could proudly lay claim to being a war correspondent and became a strong supporter of American involvement in World War I. After the United States entered the war in 1917, she obtained the support of the Creel Committee, the federal propaganda agency, to go to France to lecture for the YMCA about her experiences in Russia. She also hoped to see her son, who had enlisted, but when she sought press credentials to go to the front, she was confronted by her "old sex handicap." She persuaded American Expeditionary Force commander General John Pershing (whose sister was a newspaper editor in Lincoln) to allow her to go just behind the front lines, thus allowing her to visit her son several times before he was seriously wounded. Dorr spent many more years in Europe writing books, including her 1924 autobiography in which she celebrated the accomplishments of her generation of women and dreamed of a future that modern women can identify with. "The women of the future — the women whose feet we set on the path of progress — have a better chance to be good mothers, good wives and good citizens than we ever had." Dorr is frequently included on lists of notable historical women, often celebrated more for her advocacy for justice for working women and suffrage than the quality of her journalism. She died in Pennsylvania in 1948. Like Colby she has never been elected to the Nebraska Press Association Hall of Fame, possibly because she never practiced journalism in the state despite her roots in it.

THE FATE OF MOST WOMEN JOURNALISTS

Back in Nebraska during this period women still worked in journalism, but there were no "names" like Elia Peattie or Willa Cather. In the 1900 census 9 of the 108 Omahans listed as "reporters and editors" were women, and at least one woman, Rose Rosicky, published a paper, the Bohemian *Hospodar*. Union women also helped print the city's newspapers. However, none of the nine journalists' names appear either in a sampling of newspapers from the period or in other historical sources studied, and the *Evening World-Herald* no longer featured a bylined woman's column such as Peattie's. This seems ironic because in the first decade of the new century, Nebraska was a Progressive battleground, and women must have been especially interested in the top issues of the pivotal year 1907 such as regulating breweries and restricting child labor. Even though the state legislature waged epic battles that reshaped Nebraska that year, it was business as usual in the society sections in Lincoln's *Nebraska State Journal* and the *Evening World-Herald*.

Despite the lack of bylines, it is safe to assume that women journalists produced the social sections of Nebraska's major papers because such work had become their niche in newspapering. Examining typical issues of newspapers is an excellent way to glimpse what they were writing about and the way society viewed women. It is especially interesting to note the increased departmentalization and segmentation in papers of this era that made them far better organized and easier to read but also reminded readers of the era's rigid gender roles, especially for upper-class women. In place of Peattie's provocative, wide-ranging columns, the *Evening World-Herald* featured a Social Whirl column that provides fascinating insights into the comfortable if constrained lives of economically privileged women but never mentions the immigrant women struggling to raise families in a new world. The Social Whirl columns of the *World-Herald* and their equivalents in Lincoln portray people attending club meetings and church socials, getting married, hosting out-of-town visitors, and holding parties. The randomly selected society sections examined do not even allude to the issues of the day that had a major impact on women and families such as the fight to restrict child labor. Nor do they feature interesting and significant women or present a women's angle on issues as the 1890s papers did. Instead they offer readers an endless succession of one- and two-paragraph items with occasional long pieces on upper-class social doings such as the weddings of prominent Omahans. The contrast with the vitality of Peattie's coverage of daily life in Omaha and Dorr's society-page crusades for working women in New York is depressing.

CONTRASTING LOCAL BREVITIES WITH THE SOCIAL WHIRL

A major reason that most newspapers are so forgettable is their focus on reporting the daily community happenings of transitory interest. This was especially true at the turn of the century, when a high percentage of all news content consisted of short items that are in many ways like a community diary. Like a diary the individual items are of little interest per se, but collectively they provide a glimpse of daily life in an era for anyone willing to plow through reams of microfilm. The brief stories that offer insights into the social roles of women and men, family life, and distinctions in the way women and men are described are especially fascinating in this respect. On March 5, 1907, for example, the *Evening World-Herald* printed its Local Brevities and Social Whirl columns side-by-side, but the parallel columns depict two different faces of the city. It appears that many of the Local Brevities items originated on a police blotter than women reporters would never have examined, while male reporters would never have written items for Social Whirl. In Local Brevities items such as this juvenile-court story about a dysfunctional family, we glimpse a side of domestic life alien to Social Whirl's happy world of social events. "Judge Kennedy, sitting in juvenile court Monday, gave the custody of Dollie and Emma Chuman to the mother, who is separated from the father and suing for divorce. Chuman is now under indictment at Auburn for assault with a deadly weapon and his children, ages 11 and 7, respectively, are now here. He says he is trying to find work in Omaha." In contrast, Social Whirl reporters that day focused on two fancy parties hosted by rich people. "Mr. Tracy Cockle gave an Orpheum party Monday evening in honor of Mrs. Brown, guest of Miss Wakefield. Mr. Harry Tukey formed one of the party," and, "Mrs. John Waggaman was the guest of honor at a beautifully appointed dinner given by Mr. and Mrs. James McKenna Monday evening. Covers were laid for ten and the centerpiece was a mound of narcissus. At each place was a bunch of violets tied with a green ribbon, with the guest's name in gold. The ribbon ran from place to place, making a complete circle." Ironically both the men reporters who compiled the local briefs from the police blotter and the women society reporters who chronicled the city's endless parties wrote anonymously about mind-numbingly boring events. But the division of these items into two parallel columns suggests the parallel worlds in which male and female journalists operated, much like the sex-segregated want ads defined the division of labor between the two genders.

FIVE YEARS LATER: NEWSPAPERS LEAP FORWARD BUT NO WOMEN PHOTOJOURNALISTS

Between 1907 and 1912 newspapers changed radically in appearance and content due to advances in printing technology. Although photography had been around for more than fifty years, the typical newspaper could not print photos in 1907. By 1912, however, photos were common, drastically improving newspaper graphics, layouts, and readability. Longer stories with bigger, multicolumn headlines and darker ink replaced the dense collections of shorts in earlier papers although there were still very few bylines and photo credits. Photography opened new employment opportunities on newspapers for men but not women. Historians have determined that Nebraska's first women photographers worked in commercial photography in small towns, where there was less competition than in Omaha or Lincoln; there is no indication that any of them worked for newspapers. Ironically when a Lincoln woman finally became a photojournalist during World War II, she got her job by responding to a help-wanted ad seeking a man and was hired only because of the wartime shortage of men. Based on the sources I checked, the *World-Herald* did not hire a woman photojournalist until the mid-1970s, although women on smaller papers in Nebraska almost certainly took many of their own pictures. Some might have even been full-time photojournalists. On weekly papers woman journalists — often the copublishers — had to do all jobs, including photography, but that did not translate into such jobs opening to women in the larger cities.

Besides photography the improvements in newspapers by 1912 included expanded use of features, with more in-depth coverage of women's activities. Ironically, however, the enhanced coverage of women most likely failed to improve job opportunities for women journalists because the most substantive articles on women appeared in general news sections, not social news. The general news stories, however, reveal far more than the social shorts about the vitality of Omaha's women. In the first week of November 1912, for example, readers would have encountered everything from a YWCA investigation into the working conditions of young women to an article assuring women that nutrition was the key to good health. The November 5 YWCA story reported that the organization had hired an investigator from New York to look into the conditions under which young women labored, but the piece assured readers that the investigator was "a former Nebraska girl, her home being in Broken Bow. . . . The committee will look into the industrial conditions of young women in the different lines of work and the conditions under which they work. They will see how many have lunch rooms in connection with the places of employment, and will also try to see what other organizations are doing organized work for working young women."

Other articles in city news indicated the newspaper's awareness of women as consumers. For example, a November 6 story described the efforts of the University Club in the Board of Trade building to appeal to women. "Cretonne hangings in dainty tints will drape the windows of the women's reception and dining rooms. Furniture for the women will be reed, chairs, desk and tables being brushed in and wiped out on dark shades of green, giving an antique Pompeian effect. Portieres will be of velvet." The next day the Omaha Woman's Club received front-page coverage when a representative of a creamery told the group how his firm made butter, and a spokesmen for the Heinz Company assured the women that its vinegar was pure, adding that "the grocery man was more important than the doctor as the housewife went to the grocery man every day and to the doctor only when ill." It is interesting that all these stories appeared in city news although they would have fit the "family, food and fashion" themes of women's/social sections around the nation. It is possible that the businesses involved requested and got the more prestigious news-page story placement.

Even as city news reporters were featuring more stories targeting women in other parts of the paper, the 1912 society pages had expanded to include advice columns, recipes, fashion stories, and lavish coverage of the social lives of prominent local businessmen and their families. The *World-Herald* Social Whirl column normally began with a long item on some noteworthy social event such as the wedding plans of Charles D. Beaton, a member of the Ak-Sar-Ben Board of Governors (consisting of Omaha's business elite). A marvelous example of such coverage is this account of his nuptials:

> Among the numerous wedding gifts received by Miss Hattie Wurster and Mr. Charles Beaton is a large, plain silver platter with flowing engraving. "Presented to Mr. and Mrs. C. D. Beaton by the Board of Governors, 1912." Mr. Beaton was a member of the board of governors of the Knights of Ak-Sar-Ben and was one of the most popular members of the board. The board of governors are planning to entertain in Mr. Beaton's honor upon his return from his wedding trip, and it is not certain now whether the governors will dine alone or whether the wives will be guests of honor. Several parties have been given at Milwaukee since Mr. Beaton lived there. Miss Anna Best of that city gave a theater party Friday evening in honor of Miss Wurster and her bridal party. . . . The wedding of Miss Wurster and Mr. Beaton will take place at 6 o'clock Wednesday at the residence of the bride's parents, in the presence of the immediate families only, and will be followed by dinner and a large reception and dancing party. . . . The ceremony will be performed by Bishop (Richard) Scannell of Omaha.

This wasn't the only attention that Beaton's wedding received. The lead item of an earlier Social Whirl column had reported that Scannell was going to Milwaukee to perform the ceremony and that "Rev. Stephen Dowd [would] accompany the bishop." The November 9 Social Whirl reported that Paul Beaton and William Schnorr were the only bridal attendants from the Omaha area and listed nine Omahans attending the ceremony. "Mr. and Mrs. Beaton have planned a wedding trip to the Hawaiian Islands and will be at home in Omaha after February 1."

With Social Whirl focusing on such trivia, perhaps it makes sense that the YWCA's investigation of working conditions for young women appeared in general news. The amount of space devoted to a prominent man's wedding also suggests that perhaps the primary readers of the Social Whirl column were rich men and women rather than middle- and working-class women and that top male editors ordered the women who wrote the copy to emphasize upper-class social activities rather than covering the lives of ordinary women. This pattern appears in other eras as well, most notably the 1930s, when the women's section all but ignored the troubles of the vast majority of its women readers in favor of frothy social items about a handful of wealthy people.

WOMEN IN THE WEEKLIES

As always Nebraska women remained active in community journalism but seemingly in traditional subordinate roles. An examination of more than twenty-five volumes of Nebraska State Historical Society records of the staffs of weekly and small-town daily papers in various eras revealed the names of numerous women who assisted their husbands in running family papers. Many probably were equal partners who were not acknowledged as such. As in the Victorian era many women continued to share their husbands' careers in family businesses where the husband normally carried the top title. However, established publishers like Chattie Coleman Westenius of the *Stromsburg Headlight* continued running their papers even after they married. One note that surfaced in the hundreds of pages examined suggests how capable the women in family papers were. Albert Hammons reported that while he was away fighting in the Spanish American War in 1897, his wife and her sister, Myrtle King, ran the *Fairbury News*. Presumably Hammons regained control of the paper upon his return.

Thus as the Progressive Era ended, the career of Rheta Childe Dorr suggests that a determined young woman could leave Nebraska and crash through barriers to win unheard-of roles such as covering wars. However, those who remained in the state continued to play their established roles as independent publishers of small newspapers, partners in family journalism businesses, and traditional society section writers in larger cities. These subordinate roles mirrored the position of women in the work world and society during this era. However, the feature stories in the 1912 papers indicate that women were probably more activist than was generally acknowledged. They would demonstrate this through their work on the home front during World War I.

4 | World War I

Like many parts of the nation with large German ethnic populations, Nebraska experienced a wave of anti-German hysteria during World War I as a result of the national propaganda campaign to build support for the war. Unlike World War II, when the Pearl Harbor attack united the nation, a reason for the U.S. entry had to be defined and sold to an initially reluctant public. So successful was this campaign and the local activities it sponsored that by the time the United States entered the war in 1917, all things German became anathema, even classical music by German composers. Nebraskans responded to the campaign by trying to eradicate all evidence of their German heritage. For example, the town of Berlin near Lincoln changed its name to Otoe. The state also passed a Sedition Act requiring that materials printed in a foreign language be filed with the State Council of Defense, and after the war the legislature even passed a law aimed at German parochial schools that banned teaching any subject in any language but English. The U.S. Supreme Court declared the law unconstitutional in the important free-speech case *Meyer vs. Nebraska.*

The government propaganda effort targeted women through both the mainstream and the foreign-language press, but unlike during the Progressive Era, when their voices were seldom heard, women mobilized behind the war effort. As noted in the previous chapter, suffragists took special advantage of the anti-German sentiment to advance their cause because German American organizations had traditionally opposed woman's suffrage.

Except for Rheta Childe Dorr, who remained prominent at the

national level, no major "name" Nebraska women journalists emerged during World War I, although various documents contain scattered references to local women. So why write about the era in a book recounting the contributions of Nebraska's women journalists? The women journalists who toiled in the society sections' pages enlisted in support of World War I, left behind accounts of women engaged in home-front support efforts, and offered their readers important war-related content that help us understand life on the home front. From the state's largest papers to weeklies like the *Seward County Tribune* and the *Cedar Bluffs Standard*, society reporters turned traditional offerings such as food columns into tools for supporting the war effort as they promoted war-support activities. General news sections also saluted women's participation in the war effort as some women became auto mechanics, worked in factories, directed traffic, and harvested crops.

It is important to note that both the pro-war activism of women and the coverage such local efforts received were anything but spontaneous. For the first time in American history, the federal government mounted a massive propaganda/public relations campaign targeting its own citizens. The Committee on Public Information, better known as the Creel Committee, used everything from the movies (which were required to carry pro-war trailers) to school groups to carry the war-support message to the grassroots in every corner of the nation, including Nebraska. As soon as war was declared in 1917, each state sponsored its own Council of Defense, under the auspices of the Creel Committee, and each state council organized a woman's committee to coordinate the home-front efforts of women. From its birth on June 30, 1917, the Nebraska Woman's Committee sought to give every woman a "chance to prove her patriotism." "Our Nebraska Woman's Committee has proudly accepted this open acknowledgment by the government of the inherent right and responsibility of women to give service to their country. The women of our state as of other states labor today for the protection of their country as effectively as the soldiers fight for it on the far-flung frontiers of the war zone. Nebraska women are responding with all the vigor and unalloyed ardor which our wonderful western prairie country arouses. Our women do not talk their patriotism; they live it."

The astute strategists who ran the Creel Committee and its state affiliates understood the power of local media in shaping local public opinion. Realizing that local newspaper society sections could influence women, they cultivated these sections and targeted pro-war messages to them. It is easy to imagine that the society section writers were flattered by this attention and responded enthusiastically to requests to cover the patriotic activities of local women.

According to an official report of its activities, the Woman's Committee particularly targeted the state's foreign-language newspapers to publicize naturalization appeals "excepting only certain German publications in strongly alien districts." "Large groups of foreign born girls and women have, in response to this call, taken out their first papers as American citizens. . . . Not only have the women of Nebraska accomplished much in bringing about the Americanization of their foreign born sisters, but their activities have had a salutary effect upon the male members of the families involved. . . . Numbers of men in the families of the women seeking Americanization awoke to the realization that they too should naturalize, and forthwith they hurried to the proper authorities lest their women outdo them." These appeals may seem benign, but they occurred at a time when Congress had passed an alien act that deported thousands of immigrants whose loyalty was suspect, when the Justice Department was asking citizens to report any suspected disloyal activity, and states like Nebraska passed their own sedition acts to police possible opposition to the war. The women readers of Nebraska's foreign-language press would have been only too aware of the need to demonstrate their loyalty to their adopted country by taking out citizenship papers and pressuring their men to do the same. Whether they wanted to become citizens or not (and most probably did), they were protecting their families by doing so. On a more mundane level, the Woman's Committee also organized school Red Cross auxiliaries to involve children in knitting, making garments, and "preparing necessary supplies which [would] alleviate the suffering of our boys on the battle line," efforts local papers happily covered.

A WINDOW ON THE HOME FRONT

In examining microfilm of large and small Nebraska newspapers from this era, I was struck by the impact of the propaganda committee's work in the amount of space that they all devoted to Red Cross drives, food conservation, and other war-support efforts. The papers exhorted their readers, including women, to do their part and instructed them how to contribute. It was fascinating to see how much the tone of the coverage of women had changed in just a few years and yet how prevalent the separate spheres for women and men remained. Newspapers saluted women for getting involved but still treated them as fragile creatures needing protection. A classic example of this mentality is evident in an article in the March 28, 1917, *Evening World-Herald* under the headline "Society Women Help Recruiters during Big Rush." The accompanying article said that women "whose names figure[d] frequently in the society columns" pitched in with clerical work at the local Navy recruiting headquarters. There is one reference in the article to those women as "girls" (though all were grown women, some of them married). They were chaperoned by the wife of the naval officer in charge of the office. The next day the newspaper carried a front-page picture of four of the women dressed fashionably in broad-brimmed hats trimmed with flowers and feathers. The caption stated that they were addressing 125,000 circulars, and none of them wanted their pictures in the paper because they said they were too busy to bother with a photographer, and beside they weren't looking for publicity for themselves. They just wanted to help Uncle Sam in the only way they knew how. It seems odd that adults required a chaperone to perform a clerical task in the company of their friends. One wonders who the chaperone was protecting them from. The photographer?

Social-page mobilization behind the war effort included focusing traditional food coverage on the wartime effort to conserve food. "Watch Your Kitchen Waste. Ask Yourself—'Can It Be Eaten?'" read a headline from the May 10, 1917, *Seward County Tribune* that is typical of the many food production, preservation, and conservation messages that newspapers preached to Nebraska's women in the newspapers I examined. The *Tribune* reminded readers that "a large part of the $700,000,000 estimated food waste in this country [was] good food which [was] allowed to get into garbage pails and kitchen sinks," then offered hints for avoiding waste such as using uneaten cereal to thicken soups and gravies; using stale bread in meat dishes, desserts, and hot breads; and turning leftover meat, fish, and vegetables into patties, meat and fish pies, and other main dishes. The article reminded women that careless peeling of potatoes and fruits could waste up to 20 percent of the product. In Omaha Harriet Dakin MacMurphy's Food Talks column occupied a prominent spot in the *World-Herald* society section complete with recipes tailored to wartime restrictions. On May 3, 1918, for example, the recipes included Bean Molasses Cake, Corn Flour Griddle Cake, Barley Scones, Soy Bean Nut Bread, and Corn Flour Griddle Cakes. The Bean Molasses Cake substituted ersatz molasses (made from corn) for scarce sugar. Such adaptations helped housewives cope with national mandates to observe meatless Tuesdays and wheatless Wednesdays because the war effort needed these commodities.

The general news sections of newspapers (written by men)

featured cute stories about women so caught up in patriotic frenzy that they even tried to enter the military, but not at the cost of their femininity. An article from the March 22, 1917, *Lincoln Star* about a local young woman who sought to enlist in the navy exemplifies such coverage. "Lincoln Typist Would Become Sailorette, but Trousers — O, My," read the headline. "'Will the yeomanettes have to wear regular sailor costumes,' she asked [the navy recruiter] hesitatingly. She indicated that she might like to join the service, but would draw the line at taking a physical examination and wearing — er — ah trousers." The recruiter ducked the question, and the woman left the office "uncertain as to becoming a yeowoman in Uncle Sam's Navy."

Not all women seeking to serve were so frivolous, and the papers treated their efforts respectfully. For example, on March 6, 1917, the *Lincoln Star* reported that "Miss Helen Thiesen Would Become American Citizen for Red Cross Work." The story said that Thiesen, who had come to the United States from Germany as a child, could not become an Army nurse as she wished until completing full naturalization, but she could become a Red Cross nurse before that happened. Two days later the *Star* described a new "back to the soil movement led by women, suffrage farmerettes" sponsored by the National Woman Suffrage Association. "Lincoln suffragists were not prepared to say how far they would be willing to take the suggestion of their leaders that they replace men on the farms" to allow men to go to war. The article said that numerous women already worked on farms and gardened and that women were among humankind's first "agriculturists, using the hoe when the principal occupation of the male was to stun wild beasts with clubs and stones or brain his fellowmen when beasts weren't handy." Even this story, which treated women fairly seriously, feminizes job titles such as "farmer" when women performed the work and closes with its odd commentary on men, reminding us that society still relegated women to a separate sphere.

Nebraska newspapers strongly endorsed support for the Red Cross, the war's major social-service organization, as these typical headlines demonstrate: "Will There Be a Red Cross Candle in Your Window?" asked an ad in the December 20, 1917, *Seward County Tribune* that the paper and F. W. Goehner donated. The candle, said the ad, would tell "all who pass that you have joined the Red Cross and have sent your dollar to France to help save some wounded soldier's life or feed some starving, homeless child." "Make this a Red Cross Christmas, Your Happiness Will Be Greater." The quarter-page ad also explained that the government did not finance the Red Cross because it would cost far more to hire tax-paid workers than to mobilize volunteers. At times it is difficult to distinguish between advertising (especially when cosponsored by the paper) and news content when stories promoting Red Cross volunteerism abounded. Here is an examples of the numerous articles found in Nebraska papers that I spot-checked. "First Aid Class Formed by Omaha Society Women, 'Not Sufficient Looms to Supply Material,' Says Red Cross Director" was the headline on an article saying that the nation's mills and looms couldn't keep pace with women producing bandages and other Red Cross supplies that required fabric. The *Nebraska State Journal* published the Red Cross calendar throughout the war, printing it adjacent to traditional social items such as pictures of the Lincoln High School yearbook staff.

LOCAL SOCIETY NEWS CONTINUES

Even though soldiers were dying in the trenches of France, society pages continued to report that Nebraskans were getting married, entertaining relatives and friends, going to club meetings, and generally living their daily lives. The *Lincoln Star*, the *Nebraska State Journal*, and the *Evening World-Herald* even expanded their traditional social sections during the war years. War or no war, the *Seward County Tribune*'s Small Town Notes, for example, found room to report local social tidbits such as the visit of two women from nearby Goehner to Seward and that "Mrs. Thomas McCormick [was] quite sick at this writing." Readers also learned that "Mr. George Roth [was] building a garage at Eperspacher's" and that "quite a few from Goehner attended the play at Tamora Saturday evening." Such typical local social items filled many columns of all the social sections I reviewed, along with horoscopes, advice to the lovelorn, and serialized fiction stories. However, many otherwise traditional social section stories featured war angles in contrast with the lack of such news angles during the Progressive Era. The papers continued to advise readers on etiquette problems but now paid special attention to young women dealing with work-world problems because of the war. Cultural news remained a staple, but Nebraska's rabid anti-German sentiments even sparked an effort to ban German music from Lincoln Symphony concerts, presumably depriving music lovers of listening to Bach, Beethoven, and Brahms for the duration of the war.

A BRIDGE TO THE FUTURE

World War I is one of the most fascinating periods in American journalism history because of the impact of the government's first foray into mass propaganda in domestic coverage. The discovery that the national Creel Committee formed woman's committees in every state that, among other things, targeted immigrant women through the local foreign-language press is a small but important historical insight into the period. It reveals that the federal government reached into every facet of American life to promote the war, including small foreign-language publications in small states like Nebraska, not just that it prosecuted noted activists in New York as major histories of the era report. This use of the foreign-language press to pressure immigrant women to become American *or else* suggests that the Creel Committee's astute propagandists viewed alien women as susceptible to pressure to protect their families. The local women in the affiliates of the Creel Committee who became instruments of the national government campaign were undoubtedly well meaning, but the nation's experiment with coerced loyalty, thought control, and severe punishment of dissent remains frightening.

It is also easy to see how susceptible the bright but often ignored women who ran the local society sections would have been to appeals from the propagandists to convert their sections into war-support entities. It is easy to imagine women journalists responding enthusiastically as they saw new potential for both their sections and themselves as journalists. The Creel Committee disbanded after the war, but its impact continued for decades in the tactics that it taught advertisers about promoting their products through the women's news sections. Recipes containing brand names were featured in many food sections for years, and smart companies happily offered promotional trips to society section staff members in return for coverage, trips that regional newspapers would never have funded for low-prestige society sections. These practices were still in place in the 1970s but finally ended with that decade's radical tightening of media ethics. It is only fair to note that advertisers and corporations employed similar tactics in city news, not just society sections.

In other respects as well World War I is a bridge to the future of women in Nebraska journalism. A few had crossed into city news during the war, offering hope of greater opportunities in the coming era, when women could vote. They had started to break out of their separate sphere during the war, and the society sections had begun to reflect this movement. The anonymous women who produced these sections could look to a future where increasing numbers of them would cease to be anonymous.

5 | The Roaring Twenties & the Thirties

If you had pulled into Omaha's classic art deco Union Station in the late 1920s, you would have felt the vibe of a prosperous city adding landmarks to its skyline such as South Omaha's Livestock Exchange Building in the nation's second-largest stockyards. By now the areas near the stockyards had become a polyglot of ethnic neighborhoods representing every corner of Europe, most with their own churches still preaching in their languages of origin. However, despite the churches and its prosperity Omaha remained a rough-and-ready city where speakeasies flourished in Little Italy just blocks away from Union Station and where police winked at gambling and other organized-vice operations. Ah, the Roaring Twenties! No mere prohibition amendment to the U.S. Constitution could deprive Omahans of their pleasures.

In Lincoln it was a different story, at least when it came to prohibition. Temperance societies were a major political force, and if the twenties roared in the capital city, it was because of the championship football being played at the University of Nebraska's Memorial Stadium, where the Cornhuskers engaged in epic struggles with Knute Rockne's best Notre Dame teams. Across town the state's new capitol building, an architectural wonder of the time, was rising, a convenient fifty-mile trek by Model T for Omahans doing business with the state.

However, in rural Nebraska the only roars were cries of anguish. Between 1921 and 1923 a fourth of Nebraska's farms failed because the price of corn and wheat fell, but farmers had to repay high-interest loans on land they had bought at inflated prices during World War I. When the farmers couldn't pay their loans, country banks folded, some 650 during the decade. The coming Depression had hit Nebraska's rural areas long before Wall Street crashed in 1929, but the hard-pressed farmers could hardly imagine that even worse was to come.

In this period of winners and losers, women flourished, especially in the cities. Having won the vote, they bobbed their hair, shortened their skirts, went to college in growing numbers, and got jobs formerly closed to them. Homemakers enjoyed new appliances, and radio brought news, weather, markets, and music to a growing number of homes. Then everything crashed. By 1930 Omaha and Lincoln had discovered that they would not be spared rural Nebraska's economic pain during the Great Depression. In the wake of the financial collapse, unemployment soared, but in vintage Nebraska fashion the worst of it was the weather — years of the harshest conditions the state has ever seen that spelled economic catastrophe for farmers. Abnormally frigid winters were followed by summers of extreme drought and temperatures that soared above 100 for days on end, creating massive dust storms throughout the Midwest. As fields dried up and crops withered, Nebraska farmers grew almost nothing some years. Times became desperately hard, especially in rural areas, where hobos wandered the roads and hopped onto freight trains hoping they would arrive somewhere with jobs. Historians credit federal relief programs with keeping Nebraska afloat, but the Depression lingered throughout the decade and thousands of people fled the state when they lost their jobs, homes, and farms. Census data show that the population dropped from 1.37 million in 1930 to 1.31 million in 1940. During these hard times almost one-fifth of the population was on relief, some 250,000 people in 1938, for example. But somehow those who stayed made it through the decade of horrors, and the state itself survived these hard times.

The early 1920s were an exciting time for a young woman to launch a career in journalism in Nebraska. In Lincoln the University of Nebraska established its School of Journalism, in which about a third of the students were women who took the same demanding courses as men. In Omaha a young "flapper reporter," Bess Furman, roamed the streets in what she described in her autobiography as her "hard-used Ford," chronicling everything from bizarre crimes to colorful characters and the doings of visiting celebrities for her *Omaha Bee-News* lifestyle column. By the end of the decade, she was covering first ladies at the White House for the Associated Press. In Norfolk, Nebraska, Marie Weekes, who published the *Norfolk Press* with her husband, William, became the first woman president of the Nebraska Press Association, a highlight of her long and colorful career that gained national recognition. Meanwhile, in tiny Farnam, Nebraska, Mildred Heath began her journalistic career on the weekly *Farnam Echo*. More than eighty years later, she was still covering social news in nearby Overton at age 102.

During this expansive decade radio made its debut in the state, although it provided few opportunities for local women since the announcers who read news, weather, and sports copy were all men. In Washington DC, however, Grand Island native Grace Abbott, who headed the federal Children's Bureau, began using radio broadcasts to educate parents. As women moved into new fields and traditional women's groups spoke out on issues, Nebraska's social pages covered their expanding opportunities and changing lifestyles. However, a handful of women journalists were no longer confined to social sections and the anonymity in which most social reporters continued to labor. Nothing illustrates these breakthroughs better than the career of Bess Furman, who morphed from "flapper journalist" in Omaha into a White House reporter and eventually became a pioneer woman political reporter for the *New York Times*.

BESS FURMAN

Furman began her career by cleaning the type boxes of her father's weekly newspaper in Danbury, a small town in south-cen-

tral Nebraska, when she was only five. Although she never graduated from college, during her brief time at Kearney State
College, she edited the student paper, the *Antelope*, which led to
a job at the *Kearney Daily Hub*. Her topical poems and jingles
there attracted the attention of the *Omaha Daily News*, and in
1920 she became a feature writer for its Sunday magazine in addition to writing a weekly column. She was a star from the start.
She might have made her first appearance as what was called a
"front-page girl" on April 15, 1921, when her picture appeared
there along with a story in which she described collecting movie
gossip via long-distance telephone calls. Sometimes an especially
daring column like a "scientific survey" of the field of Omaha's
bachelors appeared under her pseudonym "Bobbie O'Dare." Furman's enjoyment of what one national writer called her "flapper
journalism" days in Omaha is evident from her description of
them in her autobiography:

> Omaha was my town — I loved every little old side street in
> it. I loved its meandering Missouri River and the prairie sun-
> sets that I rode out into, night after night, in my hard-used
> Ford. Its Little Italy, in which a murder for the honor of a
> woman marked many a Saturday night, was my delight, es-
> pecially during the annual festival for Santa Lucia. The vigor-
> ous intellectuals of its Little Bohemia often opened up for me
> vistas far beyond the inherent inlandness of Nebraska.
>
> Omaha's happenings had color and charm that make for
> good newspaper copy. A railroad cut from South Omaha
> through to the Field Club made it possible for a little Lithu-
> anian lad from the packing-house district to come hiking up
> the tracks to caddy for the local champions. He swiftly be-
> came Nebraska's greatest golfer, Johnny Goodman. One of
> our imaginative outlaws managed to manacle the pursuing
> sheriff with handcuffs intended for himself. And when the
> law got him, he escaped from prison dressed in a feminine

disguise, including a blond wig, all manufactured as his personal prison industry. These were the sort of newspapering bright bits that, taken together, made a strand strong enough to hold me in Omaha. I had looked over the East coast, and returned to Omaha by choice. I had looked over the West coast, and reserved it as the ideal spot to retire to. But now my wide native horizons were closing in on me.

A combination of Furman's talent and her disillusionment with William Randolph Hearst, whose national chain had purchased the *Bee-News*, led her to accept a job with the Associated Press in Washington DC. The turning point in her career had come in 1928, when a feature she wrote for the *Bee-News* about Al Smith's presidential campaign appearance in Omaha won a prestigious Bookman magazine award. During this same Smith campaign trip, she also met the head of AP's Washington bureau, who offered her a job there a year later. Furman's first major Washington assignment was covering a battle over the Children's Bureau headed by social worker Grace Abbott, who shared her central Nebraska roots. Their friendship helped Furman conquer her initial homesickness. "Miss Abbott was as native to me as strong breezes over wheat fields. We could talk Nebraska," Furman wrote.

As a veteran of covering the female angle of Nebraska politics, Furman was on familiar turf when AP assigned her to cover first lady Lou Hoover, who disliked publicity. One year she donned a Girl Scout uniform and joined some scouts in singing to the Hoovers in order to get a story on Christmas at the White House. Soon afterward she became the first woman to cover the House of Representatives. Continuing to cover the women's angle in presidential elections, Furman was assigned to the new first lady, Eleanor Roosevelt, after Franklin D. Roosevelt's election in 1932. A strong advocate of opportunities for women, Mrs. Roosevelt not only made a great deal of news but held women-only press conferences to encourage the hiring of women journalists. Over time Furman and her husband, journalist Robert Armstrong, whom she had married in Washington, became so close to the Roosevelts that they socialized with them and shot home movies of the first family at their Hyde Park home.

By the spring of 1937 Furman had covered President Roosevelt's landslide reelection campaign for the AP, but her concerns had become more personal. She was expecting her first child and wanted to give birth in McCook, Nebraska, where her doctor-brother could deliver the baby that turned out to be twins. She also wanted the birth certificate to reflect her "grassroots" Nebraska ties. "I not only wanted my daughter, or son, to have roots; I wanted those roots to be grassroots. I was a prairie person. . . . I had come to the conclusion that what the prairie fails to give its children in wealth, social éclat and political prestige, it makes up in a certain breezy humor and adaptability to the variable winds of life." After Robert agreed to the plan, Furman resigned from the AP and headed for McCook in western Nebraska but stopped in Omaha en route to show friends the baby blanket that Mrs. Roosevelt had knitted for her. Following the birth of Furman's twins (a girl and a boy) on April 4, the *Omaha World-Herald* carried a story about Mrs. Roosevelt's blanket that went nationwide. Postmaster General James Farley added to the excitement by ordering ten dollars' worth of flowers for Furman from a McCook florist, an order so massive that the florist had to bring more flowers by train from Omaha to fill it. This gift also made the papers. Furman's next challenge was returning to Washington with her twins in the midst of a dust bowl summer. With the help of her brother, she bundled up the babies to protect them from a massive dust storm that swept through the prairies during the long drive back to Washington. Later she reflected that this experience had given her son and daughter "their native and inevitable Nebraska baptism of grit."

After Furman returned to Washington, she and her sister, Lucile, started a freelance writing service, but during World War II she joined the Office of War Information, where she produced publications such as *War Jobs for Women*, which was distributed to more than fifty thousand people. In 1943 she joined the *New York Times* as a pioneer female political reporter for that paper and left it to head the press information section of the Department of Health, Education, and Welfare during the Kennedy administration. She retired in 1963 and died in 1969. Furman's career was so distinguished that unlike Peattie, she did not have to wait decades for recognition from Nebraska's journalistic community. She is generally acclaimed as Nebraska's greatest female journalist and one of the greatest journalists of either sex to claim roots in the state; in 1975 she was elected a charter member of the Nebraska Press Association Hall of Fame, and in 2011 she became a charter member of the Nebraska Federation of Press Women Hall of Fame. In addition to her 1949 autobiography, *Washington By-Line*, she wrote *White House Profile*, a book about the nation's first ladies, many of whom she had covered. Her papers covering the years 1928–67 are in the Library of Congress. They include her diaries, family papers, general correspondence, speeches, and writing.

A "FIGHTING WOMAN PUBLISHER" FROM NORFOLK

While Furman showed how far a woman from a small town in Nebraska could go in national journalism, Marie Weekes demonstrated that a weekly journalist could win national recognition without leaving the state. In her 1936 book on notable women journalists, Ishbel Ross pays Weekes this tribute: "Nebraska has a fighting woman publisher too, in Mrs. Marie Weekes, who has put over many a campaign in the quarter of a century that she has been a successful country editor in Norfolk, Nebraska."

Weekes was born on a farm and taught before becoming a reporter and a "hand compositor" on a local newspaper. Once when her colleagues had gone off to a "jamboree," she produced the paper herself. After moving from town to town launching and running papers, she and her journalist husband, William, moved to Norfolk and started their paper, competing with three other weeklies in the town of about seven thousand people. Although the Weekeses' paper was politically independent, Marie ran for Congress in 1920 as a farmer-labor candidate, the same year that she was a William Jennings Bryan delegate to the Democratic Convention. "She made a picturesque campaign and although the Harding landslide swept the Republican candidate to victory, she carried several counties without aid of a party label." Weekes was especially active 1924, when in addition to serving as president of the Nebraska Press Association, she cofounded the Nebraska Writers Guild, whose members included the distinguished novelists Willa Cather and Bess Streeter Aldrich. In 1931, four years after her husband's death, Marie Weekes sold the family paper, and by 1936 she had become Norfolk's postmaster.

Ross's book cites the advantages that writers for weeklies enjoyed, including a "freedom of expression denied the metropolitan reporter" and the ability to "continue at her job until she is eighty years of age, if her eyesight is good and she so desires." No one ever took more advantage of this last opportunity than Mildred Heath of Overton, Nebraska, who was still writing her weekly column as a centenarian and traveled to Washington DC in 2008 to accept an award as the nation's oldest journalist.

NATION'S OLDEST JOURNALIST RECALLS THE 1920S AND 1930S

While Bess Furman was driving around Omaha during the 1920s seeking spicy "Bobbie O'Dare" items for her columns, Mildred Heath spent her days walking up and down the streets of Farnam (pop. 394 in 1930) seeking items for hers in the *Farnam Echo*. She covered everything but sports in this Dawson County community west of Kearney as well as performing every task required to publish her weekly when occasion demanded it. She not only gathered information but also covered events, took photos, and wrote stories in addition to producing the paper mechanically. Heath thought nothing of setting her stories in type on the big, old linotype machine, fitting the metal "hot-type" stories, headlines, and photo engravings into a page frame, then casting the type into page plates that she installed on the press.

Mildred had mastered the production skills early in her career on the *Echo*, which she joined in 1923. Her future husband, Blair, whom she met at Curtis High School, also worked there. Eventually the two married and bought the *Echo* in 1927, but they moved to nearby Overton (population about 600) in 1938 after residents asked them to come and reopen the town's closed newspaper. Blair named the new paper the *Overton Observer*, and the two produced it as a team. However, due to Blair's frequent illnesses from a thyroid condition, Mildred often put out the paper single-handedly.

In 2010 Mildred still lived in Overton and still wrote for the paper. When I interviewed her in 2009 at age 101, she had no difficulty talking on the phone or re-creating the world of weekly journalism in rural Nebraska eighty-five years ago. She particularly recalled how "terribly hard" the times were in the state's cash-starved small towns. When customers did not have the money to pay for their subscriptions, they sometimes paid the Heaths with a couple of chickens or homegrown produce. A local weekly paper in Nebraska cost about seventy-five cents a year in the 1930s, but many people couldn't afford even that.

Like most Nebraska weekly editors, the Heaths supplemented their income by printing items like sale handbills and programs. The dust storms of the 1930s meant constant additional cleaning but didn't interfere with printing either the paper or the extras since the press was in a back room with only one window. The family saved money by living in its newspaper production plant, an arrangement that also helped Mildred juggle putting out the paper and raising her three daughters. This was especially handy on Tuesdays, when the paper went to press to meet its Wednesday mailing deadline for rural subscribers. Production days would start at 8:00 a.m. and sometimes last until 2:30 a.m. the next day. Often late Tuesday nights would find Mildred, clad in overalls, standing on a box and hand-feeding paper into the press until the wee hours. It comforted her to know that her girls were sleeping just rooms away and could easily contact her no matter how late. When the girls were older, they helped produce the newspaper, coercing at least one of their suitors, Norman Taylor, into helping. Taylor later joked that he came to see daughter Polly, and Mildred put him to work for many years. Eventually he married Polly and took over running the newspaper. In 1972 he and Polly merged the *Overton Observer* with the nearby Elm Creek paper and named the merged paper the *Beacon-Observer*, which still covers this corner of Dawson County, although the Heath family no longer owns it.

Throughout her life in addition to her newspaper work, Heath was a fixture of the Daughters of the American Revolution, the Methodist Church Women, and the National Rifle Association. She said she kept working because her eyesight, hearing, and health remained good, and she could see no reason to retire as long as she loved what she was doing. "I've had a wonderful life."

JOURNALISM EDUCATION AT THE UNIVERSITY OF NEBRASKA

Journalism in Nebraska received a boost in 1923 when the University of Nebraska transferred journalism education from the English department to its new School of Journalism, which raised the status of journalism instruction and symbolized the field's growing professionalism. The university's move was consistent with national trends and recognized that students were studying to become writers and editors in contrast to earlier generations of journalists, who had usually been either printers or affiliated with political parties. From the start women participated fully in the journalism program, unlike in numerous other schools that offered separate courses for women. A check of University of Nebraska bulletins in the 1920s showed that from the start, about a third of the school's students were women, roughly their percentage in the student body at the time. There is also no evidence that women used a text "designed exclusively for women students" to prepare them to cover news from "a woman's view-point" nor any courses listed that sound as if they were designed for women. The bulletins show that women took the same required courses as men, including Journalism 171, which prepared students to cover police, courts, and local government. This legendary course was a linchpin of the curriculum for generations and remains an indelible memory for the alums who took it as recently as the 1960s. Thus from the beginning "J-School" made equal demands on all students, a policy that enhanced the careers of generations of women students. However, the early journalism program was oriented toward weekly papers, and it offered courses in small-town and country journalism, including one on how to bid printing jobs. Students who did not know how to type were required take a typing course from Teachers College.

THE BIRTH OF RADIO IN NEBRASKA

Even though the University of Nebraska School of Journalism was created in the same decade that radio took root in the state, the initial instructional focus was strictly print oriented. This reflected the fact that although Nebraska newspapers were among the sponsors of the radio stations that had started popping up around the state during the 1920s and early 1930s, it took years for most of them to practice serious journalism. Stations came and went rapidly, and some were little more than amateur hobby operations or class projects at places like Omaha's Commerce High School. A few of these pioneer stations are still in existence although not always in the same location. One thing that all early Nebraska radio stations seem to have had in common was the male gender of their staffs. A master's thesis on the early days of

Omaha radio lists no women being involved in local radio, and James Potter, senior research historian for the Nebraska State Historical Society, states that the earliest women featured on Nebraska radio stations were entertainers, mostly singers. Some of them might have appeared with young future movie star Robert Taylor when he began his radio career at KMMJ in Clay Center. The station later moved to Grand Island, where it still broadcasts.

Nebraska's radio stations might have been run by men, but Grand Island native Grace Abbott became a national pioneer in using radio to educate the public when she headed the federal Children's Bureau. She and her staff began delivering weekly radio talks on child health and welfare in 1922. She later recalled, "We did not want to print reports which the social historian might read some 100 years from now and say the investigation was well made, and the recommendations valuable, and it was too bad nobody ever heard anything about it at the time the report was made. For this reason the Bureau has sought by presentation of scientific material in popular bulletins, in motion pictures, and in the press to reach the public which must be reached to accomplish results in the promotion of child health and child welfare. When broadcasting by radio was possible, we recognized in it a new means of accomplishing this end." The bureau broadcast its first programs from the navy station in Washington, but Abbott, who did not own a radio, had trouble gaining access to them. Finally when she went to a Washington store to try to hear a broadcast, a clerk fiddled with a radio, seeking the navy station but gave up, saying, "Well lady, this ain't what you want anyways. It's a child health program."

Abbott stopped broadcasting for a time, but later the bureau sponsored weekly talks on CBS and NBC. She was among the first to urge government-sponsored educational radio, arguing, "We cannot hope to combine amusement and education for adults and improve the programs for children unless program-making is carefully studied by someone other than advertisers." Eventually Abbott turned most of the bureau's actual broadcasts over to her staff because the work was so time consuming, but she merits recognition for her groundbreaking use of the medium for educational purposes.

HARD TIMES HIT NEBRASKA JOURNALISM

Nebraska's newspapers suffered along with everything else during the Depression with many folding or merging with competitors. In 1917 the number of Nebraska's newspapers reached an all-time high of seven hundred. However, during the 1920s and 1930s small towns frequently lost one of their two newspapers, according to State Historical Society records. Competition also declined in the cities. In Omaha in 1937 Hearst sold the *Bee-News* to the *Omaha World-Herald*, which then folded it, while in Lincoln the *Nebraska State Journal* and the *Lincoln Star* merged their business operations and started publishing a combined Sunday edition in 1931 to prevent both from going broke. Employees felt the hardship, including women like Lois Dwiggins Weyand, who started her job on the *Journal*'s "bride desk" in 1929. Her job required not only writing for the paper but occasionally modeling as a bride in photos for her section. In 1933 she became society editor, making twenty dollars a week until her pay was cut by three dollars a week due to the Depression. She considered herself fortunate to keep her job because many women, especially those who were married, lost their jobs and felt society's hostility toward their desire to work.

During the Depression many people believed that women, especially married women, unfairly deprived men of jobs that they should have had. Women lost their jobs faster than men as employers, including the federal government, fired "secondary wage earners" to keep heads of household employed. Teachers who married often lost their jobs, a trend that began in the 1920s and accelerated during the Depression. Women sometimes remained single or married secretly just to stay employed as evidenced by the fact that during the 1930s, 92 percent of Nebraska's teachers were single. In 1930 women had made up about 22 percent of the nation's workforce, being heavily concentrated in occupations such as teaching, clerical work, and domestic service. These sex segregated employment patterns eventually helped women regain their jobs sooner than men because few worked in heavy industry, which the Depression hit hardest. Later, however, men benefited far more than women from New Deal protection of union jobs that paid higher wages because few of the women-dominated service jobs were unionized. It is difficult to find any statistics about the Depression's impact on women in journalism, especially in Nebraska, because of the modest numbers involved, but national trends suggest what was happening. Weyand's story is quite likely indicative of the experience of many of Nebraska's society page writers, while wives working in family-owned newspapers that failed shared the hardships of their husbands.

One way that women journalists retained their jobs was to own a successful paper like Chattie Coleman Westenius of Stromsburg. In 1932 she celebrated her fortieth anniversary of editing the *Stromsburg Headlight* by publishing a book about the town's history. The Nebraska Press Association's newsletter saluted this achievement: "For nearly two years, short historical sketches of Stromsburg were run as featured in the *Headlight*. After each feature had been published in the newspaper, Mrs. Westenius had had a number of copies printed on uniform book size paper. These pages were carefully filed away. After more than two years of continuous accumulation of this material, Mrs. Westenius assembled it and had a number of volumes bound in book form. The book contains 190 pages and more than 200 articles."

WOMEN IN THE NEWS, 1926 VERSUS 1936:
A TALE OF TWO MIRRORS

For this period as for all the eras examined in this book, I sampled issues of Nebraska newspapers to see what they reflected

about their decades. In this instance, as in others, the exercise
was revealing, perhaps more so in these two decades than any
others examined because of the significant contrasts in the social
sections. If the social pages can be viewed as a window into the
lives of women, the differences in the contents of the *Evening
World-Herald*'s social pages during the first two weeks of July
1926 and July 1936 might be dubbed "A Tale of Two Mirrors." Although some things about the social sections in all eras remain
constants, the 1926 paper reflects women entering new careers,
playing sports, and speaking out politically in addition to getting
married, entertaining, and raising families. In contrast the July
1936 social sections might almost be a fun-house mirror, so dis-
torted is their depiction of the lives of most Nebraska women
struggling to survive the nadir of the dust bowl and the Depression. Depression? What Depression? Dust bowl? What dust bowl?
The "burning" question in the society section seemed to be how
to entertain at the country club despite heat that soared to 110
day after day. The closest to reality the section came was a few
reader suggestions on how to beat the heat. The society sections
from the two decades speak volumes about the advances women
made in the 1920s and the setbacks they suffered in the thirties,
even if they were rich women enjoying a privileged life while the
masses struggled to stay afloat. Ultimately responsibility for the
content of all sections of the paper rests with top management
rather than the rank and file journalists who carry out orders. It
would be interesting to know if the society reporters suggested
harder-hitting stories, or if they feared that arguing increased
their own vulnerability to being laid off.

THE 1926 MIRROR: WOMEN ON THE MOVE

In 1926 the *World-Herald* social section still featured a Social Affairs column recounting the comings and goings of prominent
local people, while In Cupid's Nest still offered details about their
weddings. Numerous other short items described parties, pic-

nics, and vacation plans and listed out-of-town guests. But headlines, stories, and photos both in the society and the news sections also provided a view of active women hardly imaginable
several decades earlier as these samples illustrate. For example,
"Woman Student at Nebraska Medical College Will Be Interne
at Douglas County Hospital" reported on the achievements of
an aspiring woman doctor, a story that would have been unthink-
able a decade earlier. The story reported, "For the first time in
the history of Nebraska Medical College, a junior internship has
been granted a woman. She is Charlotte Mitchell of David City,
Neb." Mitchell said she was excited by the opportunity to work
in "the insane wards that few general hospitals provide" as well
as with X-rays, new technology in which most students received
only theoretical instruction.

The growing business and political clout of recently enfran-
chised women is evident in the story "Business Women Will Enjoy Fourth" describing the plans of the Omaha Business and Professional Women's Club to attend the organization's national
convention in Des Moines, which would "concern itself with the
shaping of future national policies touching women in business."
This piece is fascinating because it is so matter of fact in reporting that (1) such a group exists and that (2) these women assumed
that they should have a voice in making national policy that
would affect them. Suffragist journalists such as Clara Bewick
Colby, who had viewed economic and political empowerment
as inseparable from each other, would have been thrilled to read
pieces like this. Similarly some stories such as "Girls Rid Wheat
Field of Parasites" showed girls in more-active roles than had articles in earlier eras. This piece reported that two Bennington,
Nebraska, girls in a wheat field had "spent the whole day . . .
plucking out every shoot of rye, so the wheat would show the
highest possible degree of perfection when inspected before har-
vest by University of Nebraska experts."

There was new recognition of working women even in traditional social stories such as an engagement announcement headlined "Miss Swartzlander of Library Staff to Wed." Focusing on the prospective bride's professional accomplishments, it said, "She is widely known for her years of service in the Omaha public library and the interest she has taken in children's books. Miss Swartzlander is now in charge of the South Omaha branch library."

The paper as a whole recognized the careers and achievements of women as illustrated by a fascinating feature from a Sunday Magazine focusing on the work of telephone operators. The piece was headlined "The Girls Who Telephone Your Telegraph Messages," with the subhead "They Convey News of Grief and Joy by Day and Night," hinting at the human dramas in which operators sometimes participated when they saved lives by connecting people with help. Acting in some cases like today's 911 operators, they handled emergencies as well as conveying joyous news of births. I'll overlook calling these adult operators "girls."

> Out in the sand-hill country a woman lay at the point of death recently. A doctor telegraphed to Omaha for "a consultation by wire" with a local specialist. But this doctor, like a great many others, was hard to find. But one of these girls [telephone operators] got busy with the phone, she called place after place until she finally got him. In 27 minutes, the deed was done. The consultation was wired back, and the woman still lives and is getting along fine. When it's a boy the message is phoned to daddy. "Oh Boy," "Hot Sam," and other jubilant expressions are among the words that are not counted in the [telegraphed] reply. Papas always relish congratulations and these girls give it free of change.

Note, however, the article's blatant sexism in reporting on the way fathers reacted to the birth of a son versus that of a daughter. That said, hardly a day passed in which the paper did not inform readers about something active women were doing, whether it was accepting a job with the YWCA in Argentina, being admitted to the YMCA's business and technical classes for the first time, or introducing readers to an Ak-Sar-Ben duchess (a young woman from a socially prominent family) who was learning to shoot a rifle from a facedown position. Contrast this with social women who could only stuff envelopes for World War I navy recruiting under the supervision of a chaperone. Women even made a few appearances in the sports section by competing in tennis, and it was obviously acceptable for them to be interested in sports such as boxing as a July 10, 1926, front-page feature demonstrated. In an interview visiting movie star Madge Bellamy predicted that Jack Dempsey would defeat Gene Tunney in their upcoming heavyweight boxing title fight, which she said she looked forward to attending. In short the society sections of the 1926 *World-Herald* have a startlingly modern vibe that, sad to say, subsequently disappears for many years. Certainly the social sections of the same paper a decade and a world later could hardly be more revealing about the decline in the status of women during the Depression.

THE 1936 MIRROR: WHAT DUST BOWL AND DEPRESSION?

The social sections from July 1936 were especially interesting because I grew up hearing family stories about the horrors of that month and year, especially for the state's farmers. That month brought record high temperatures and extreme drought, probably the worst few weeks of the Depression for many Nebraskans. I was curious if the coverage of the lives of women would bear any relationship to these stories of the horrifying heat, the utter devastation of the crops, and the suffering of people who lost their jobs, farms, and homes. The contrast between the social sections and what most survivors remember is shocking. While most accounts of Nebraska in the 1930s in the news sections of papers, including the *World-Herald*, focused on the horrors and hardships, the society pages scarcely noted them. Gone are the female medical interns and the rifle-shooting socialites to say nothing of businesswomen hoping to influence national policy. While Nebraska women who recorded their memories for books on the dust bowl like *The Dirty Thirties* remembered years of "Nothing but Hard Work and Do Without," as one chapter is aptly titled, a July 5, 1936, society story, "Getting Around — at Seventeen," describes what must have seemed like a fantasy world to most readers, who were just trying to survive. "Seen through the kaleidoscope of gay summer events Wednesday night at the Blackstone were Sally Smith and Virginia Austin doing a little Rockford reminiscing over lemon cokes; Suzie Roeder and Bob Fuch enjoying some of Jay Ramsey's tales about Grinnell and Bob Rogers, home from New Mexico military institute with Myrtle Newbranch who was telling of her future trip to Europe." How far removed were these privileged young people from my grandmother on a drought-stricken farm in Ulysses, Nebraska, struggling to feed not only her family of seven people but to find something to share with wandering men who came to her door begging for food.

News section headlines told of local highs of 110 on July 3, the highest temperature ever recorded in July and close to an all-time record. Two days later readers learned that Omaha had hit 110 again, while LeMars, Iowa, reached 117. Even though photos in the news section during these two weeks depicted dying crops and headlines told of Catholics praying for rain, the July 11 society page had other concerns. "Hostesses Seek Cool of Country Club and Hotel Dining Rooms for Their Midsummer Entertaining," read a headline over a story listing upcoming society luncheons. The same section featured the column Travelers and Newcomers and numerous photos of smiling well-dressed women. Again, I think of the hungry "travelers" who appeared at Grandma McGowen's door begging for a meal.

Not all Omaha newcomers made the social section. A few appeared in the news sections because of their connection with the ominous events unfolding in Nazi Germany. A chilling headline and story in the news section told the story of Mr. and Mrs. Eric Steinberg, "Forsake Fortune in Reich, Seek New Start in Omaha." Steinberg, a formerly wealthy manufacturer, had fled the Nazis even though it meant leaving his fortune behind to join Mrs. Steinberg's Creighton dental-student brother in Omaha. Modern readers realize the fate the family would have suffered if it had not chosen personal safety over financial catastrophe. Ironically on July 14 a local Jewish business leader, city commissioner Harry Trustin, was featured in a society section story about a luncheon and dance honoring his departure for an extended trip to Europe. One wonders where he went and if he encountered relatives or other coreligionists threatened by the specter of the Nazis' growing power. Was he possibly trying to encourage some of them to flee or covertly trying to arrange this? Could this have been a reason for his extended trip?

As if to provide at least a little balance to photos of wealthy young women cooling off at exclusive swimming pools, the society section carried some stories offering readers' heat-beating suggestions. Tips included chilling bedding in the refrigerator, bathing in Epsom salts, and sleeping with a horsehair pillow refrigerated for six hours before bedtime. The society section also carried numerous stories on a jelly-making contest that it was sponsoring with Hayden's Store. Food writer Nadine Bradley, who received the only local byline in the section, also planned to conduct a three-day jelly-making school that would "give many pointers that [would] prove valuable to both veterans and novices in the homemaking field." Bradley's stories seemed to offer some small balance in a section heavily tilted to the privileged. On July 14, 1936, for example, she reported the impact of the extreme heat on fruit supplies for canning. "Quality is not good and price is high. It is expected that peaches and apricots will come closest to being the cheap fruits for this year, but the season for these is not far enough advanced to be certain." Incidentally it speaks volumes about the status of women journalists at the time that efforts to learn more about Bradley proved futile.

Unfortunately it is impossible to interview Bradley and her female colleagues who produced these unreal social sections to learn the story behind their stories because presumably they are dead. They could scarcely have risked making waves any more than male colleagues at the *Omaha World-Herald* who lived through those awful years. In the 1970s during lunch conversations, they would reminisce about the relief they felt when they merely suffered pay cuts but kept their jobs. One or two were *Bee-News* veterans who remained grateful to the *World-Herald* for hiring them after their paper closed.

6 | The 1940s

The opening of the 1940s brought no sudden improvement to drought- and Depression-stricken Nebraska. By 1940 population had dropped about 60,000 to 1.31 million, and the summers of 1940 and 1941 were among the driest on record. There were reasons for hope, however. The number of Nebraskans on public assistance fell about 25,000 between 1938 and 1942, while manufacturing increased but not to the level of 1929. Football fans rejoiced when the Cornhuskers were invited to play Stanford in the 1941 Rose Bowl, and university students interrupted classes for an impromptu march through downtown Lincoln on the day of the announcement. Although Nebraska lost the bowl game, that defeat seemed far less significant a year later following the December 7, 1941, attack on Pearl Harbor. Like the rest of the nation, Nebraska would never be the same after the American entry into World War II. During the next four years, about 120,000 Nebraskans served in the armed forces, and some 3,839 lost their lives. On the home front Nebraska's greatest contribution to the war effort was agricultural, thanks to the return of rain, but the state also housed military bases and prisoner-of-war camps in addition to some war industries. Bellevue (just south of Omaha) was the site of the Glenn Martin aircraft assembly plant, which built the B-29s that dropped the first atomic bombs on Hiroshima and Nagasaki. At its peak the plant employed 14,500 workers. After the war the U.S. Air Force took over the site for Offutt Air Force Base, headquarters of the Strategic Air Command during the cold war and today's Strategic Command.

Throughout the war Nebraskans bought war bonds, raised victory gardens, collected scrap metal, and volunteered for the Red Cross and the uso. Although both the government and the media constantly exhorted citizens to assist the war effort, there was no need for a massive domestic propaganda campaign to engineer political support for a war that nearly everyone agreed had to be fought. No communities anywhere did more for servicemen and women than North Platte and surrounding towns. Volunteers at the acclaimed North Platte Canteen provided sandwiches and home-baked treats daily for three thousand to five thousand service members throughout the war during their brief stopover at the Union Pacific Depot. Although the depot has been demolished, the canteen has been immortalized in documentaries and books based on the memories of canteen workers and the servicemen and women they entertained.

Any discussion of women during World War II conjures images of Rosie the Riveter, for between 1940 and 1945 the nation's female labor force expanded by 5.5 million. By war's end 38 percent of all women sixteen and over were working. But the "Rosie" images can be misleading, especially in states such as Nebraska. Although the federal government sponsored public relations campaigns to encourage women to join the armed forces or replace men in factories, the public never fully accepted the ideas. A 1945 Roper poll found that 60 percent of the respondents opposed women taking jobs because their place was in the home with the strongest opposition coming from the Plains states. The thousands of women who responded to the government's call to arms or the factories were the strongest supporters of such participation in the war effort. In professions such as journalism, the war offered women opportunities to fill jobs normally held by men such as city news reporting and news photography. However, like other "Rosies" in all sorts of fields nationwide, many Nebraska women journalists found that their employers considered them a temporary wartime necessity to be dispensed with as rapidly as possible after the war ended. Statistics show that between 1945 and 1947, the percentage of professional jobs that women held fell 6 percent. By 1947 women held just under 40 percent of the nation's professional jobs but those included teachers and nurses. Some women quit their jobs voluntarily to raise families, but others were fired to give way to returning veterans. Many of Nebraska's "Rosie the Reporters" who remained in the field after the war had no choice but to return to traditional female jobs in social news after a few heady years of covering practically everything. Some would remain in journalism long enough to take advantage of the new opportunities that opened to women thirty years later. They were among the "Rosies" in many occupations who never forgot what they had accomplished during the war and the satisfaction they felt from contributing to the nation's victory. Some historians believe that the war memories of these women planted the seeds for the women's movement of the early 1970s.

The Nebraska to which Johnny and Jane came marching home from World War II was far more prosperous than the state they had left. Many veterans took advantage of the G.I. Bill to enter college, thus fueling the growth of higher education in the state, while others found jobs that opened in a newly prosperous economy or returned to their farms to enjoy several years of decent growing conditions. Families spent their war savings on cars and appliances, including that popular new invention the television set. Omaha became one of the first cities in the region to have two TV stations before 1950, and a few women were among the state's pioneers in broadcasting. Towns built new schools to accommodate the massive baby-boom generation and invested in the hospitals, highways, parks, and pools demanded by the veterans and their families. Like the nation Nebraska had come a long way from the grimmest days of the Great Depression.

World War II opened news jobs to women that they had seldom held, including going to the front as war correspondents. Nationally some one hundred women became accredited war correspondents, but when I studied an authoritative account of these women, I could find none with Nebraska ties. As nearly as I can determine, Nebraska's "Rosie the Reporters" all served on the home front, but many filled jobs that would otherwise have been closed to them, including Marj Paxson and Betty Craig of United Press's all-female wartime statehouse bureau; Mae Eden, the only photographer for the *Lincoln Journal* and the *Lincoln Star*; and Marie Dugan, the wire editor of the *Lincoln Journal* who selected and edited the paper's national and international stories. The *World-Herald* apparently employed at least a few women in city news, although I found no women's bylines in the numerous wartime editions that I examined, and no one I interviewed remembered their names. A deceased editor had told me years ago that the paper had hired a couple of women during the war but fired them after it ended because they had caused unspecified difficulties. To avoid any similar problems, the paper then kept women out of city news for twenty years, he told me. (During my research for this book, one person told me that the problems that led women to be barred from news jobs included one female reporter's affair with a male news-staff member, but I cannot confirm this.) In North Platte Bonnie Reitan had a front seat on history by covering the Canteen for the *North Platte Telegraph* and volunteering for it as well, while small-town editors such as Ruth Best Pagel of Neligh ran their family newspapers in collaboration with their husbands. Pagel actually had her greatest impact on Neligh during the postwar years of recovery and rebuilding. Of all of Nebraska's "Rosie the Reporters," Paxson's career best illustrates the nontraditional work that women journalists performed during World War II.

MARJ PAXSON

When Paxson got a job with United Press (UP) covering Nebraska state government during World War II, she was required to sign a standard agreement "acknowledging that [she] had taken a

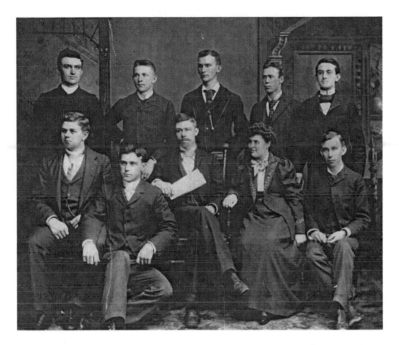

1. Novelist Willa Cather began her career in journalism at the University of Nebraska. She is shown here with the *Hesperian* staff while she was a student. (Archives and Special Collections, University of Nebraska–Lincoln)

2. Bess Furman gained national fame for covering Eleanor Roosevelt for the AP and for her government reporting for the *New York Times*. Here she shows off her book of memoirs, *Washington By-Line*. (Courtesy of Nebraska Press Women)

3. Women working in a Nebraska newsroom in 1897 show that they had gained a toehold in this mostly male field before the turn of the century. (Courtesy of Nebraska State Historical Society, RG3831-PH-1-19)

4. This photo (date not recorded) shows the *World-Herald*'s Women's News Department

when it was just that. (Reprinted with permission from the *Omaha World-Herald*)

5. Even when the *World-Herald* began to modernize, women's news reporters worked in their own area of the newsroom with no men for years. (Reprinted with permission from the *Omaha World-Herald*)

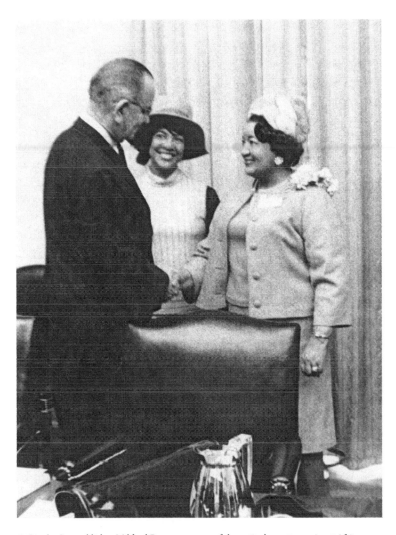

6. *Omaha Star* publisher Mildred Brown was one of the nation's most prominent African American journalists. She is shown here with President Lyndon B. Johnson. (Courtesy of Nebraska State Historical Society, RG5503-PH-0-3)

7. Editor Patricia Wolfe transformed the *Omaha World-Herald*'s women's news section into a more broadly based Living features section employing both women and men. (Reprinted with permission from the *Omaha World-Herald*)

8. Beverly Deepe covered not only the war in Vietnam but the lives of its people like these Vietnamese children she is interviewing. (Associated Press)

9. Linda Beermann was best known as KOLN/KGIN-TV's weather reporter, as this promotional ad shows, but she covered a wide range of stories and served as assignment editor. (Courtesy of Allen and Linda Beermann)

10. Janet Poley, who became a noted leader in distance education, began her career by producing and hosting Nebraska ETV's program *House and Home*. (Courtesy of Janet Poley)

11. Lynne Grasz, who became an executive at CBS, began her broadcasting career at NU's FM station KNUS, where she served as news director. She's shown here working at the station in 1964. (Courtesy of Lynne M. Grasz)

12. Pioneer consumer reporter Trudy Lieberman has returned to the University of
Nebraska College of Journalism to teach occasional advanced reporting classes.
(Courtesy of College of Journalism and Mass Communications, University of
Nebraska–Lincoln)

13. Mary McGrath became an award-winning medical reporter for the
Omaha World-Herald after transferring to city news from the Women's News
Department. (Courtesy of the Omaha Press Club Foundation Board)

man's job because he had gone off to war and agreeing to give it up when he came back." At the end of the war when it was enforced, Paxson did not protest, but she was not happy about it. "As soon as the war was over, out the women went; you were out. The only kinds of jobs that women could get in newspapers were in the society section," said Paxson in an oral-history interview covering her career. For a few years she had gained valuable experience, showing that she could cover anything, which she used when she returned to news later in her career.

The wartime shortage of men had made it easy for Paxson to land her UP job in Nebraska following her graduation from the University of Missouri's journalism program. After a short orientation in Omaha, she joined statehouse bureau manager Marguerite Davis in covering the governor, the legislature, and even the state high school basketball tournament and other sports. "We covered track meets. The men who were around were very helpful. The sports editor of the *Lincoln Journal*, where our office was, was a big help." At first Paxson was "a little bit undone" when she found she would be working for a woman because "women just weren't supposed to be bosses," but Davis "just turned out to be terrific." Paxson had believed that because of her Missouri journalism degree, she knew everything, but Davis and her assignments taught her that she still had a lot to learn. At the Nebraska Supreme Court, for example, she learned about sexual harassment because the clerk "liked the ladies." She recalled, "He liked to pat you and stuff like that. And Marguerite had warned me to 'just keep your distance.' And I found out about the second time that I went in there to pick up Supreme Court decisions—because he came around from the other side of his desk and put his arms around me. I tried to move away and he was following me through the stacks."

Paxson's job included operating the bureau's teletype machine, and her assignments kept her "running all the time," but she experienced a few restrictions due to her sex. The United Press's

Omaha bureau manager, who oversaw the Lincoln bureau, refused to let her and Davis cover executions at the state penitentiary. "He just didn't think women should cover that," Paxson
said. "Now there might have been a penitentiary regulation but
I really don't think so. I think this was just his feeling." Nor could
Paxson and Davis cover NU football games because the university banned women from the Memorial Stadium pressroom, a
restriction that continued until the 1960s. Much of Paxson's job
involved rewriting stories from the Lincoln papers for transmis-
sion to other newspapers in Nebraska. The bureau covered no
war news until the war had ended and the War Department gave
wire services the names of POWs freed by the Japanese rather
than contacting the families individually. All three news services
with bureaus in Nebraska competed to call families of former
prisoners from the state, resulting in some extremely happy families and some strong news stories.

When the war ended, Paxson lost her job to a man with no
experience when the man who had held it before the war did not
reclaim it. United Press fired her and forty-five other women in
its central region during the same week in the fall of 1946 as a
cost-cutting move because pay was based on experience regardless of sex. The man who replaced Paxson earned twenty dollars
a week less due to his lack of experience. Soon afterward she
found a job with the Associated Press in Omaha writing radio
wire copy. "Basically the radio wire was rewriting the news stories and then putting together reports of the weather forecasts,
the livestock markets, these kinds of things that in an agricultural
state all the farmers wanted to hear on the 12 o'clock news." Two
years later she became society editor of the *Houston Post* and
eventually finished her career as publisher of a Gannett newspaper in Oklahoma. Her oral history, part of a national collection
that preserves the memories of significant female journalists,
provides great insights into the daily life of women reporters on
the home front in regional communities such as Lincoln.

ONE-WOMAN PHOTO STAFF

While the all-female Lincoln UP bureau was sending stories out over the teletype, photographer Mae Eden was on call twenty-four hours a day, seven days a week to supply both Lincoln papers with photos throughout the war. Because she was the only local photographer for the papers, the calls came at all hours of the day and night. Even with all the pressures, Eden loved the job. Once when she got paid, she told herself, "All this and heaven too?" By modern standards the pay was modest, just eighty-six dollars for salary and expenses during a typical two-week period. Some of Eden's love for this demanding job may reflect her realization that she wasn't even supposed to be considered for it: she had landed it by responding to a help-wanted advertisement for a man at a time when the want ads were sex segregated. She applied because she had nothing to lose by trying, and she thought she had a chance. "Men were being drafted. I'd studied journalism at Union College (in Lincoln) and it sounded like fun. That helps," she said years later. Eden's colleagues appreciated her efforts. "She was a fine photographer and carried a heavy load," said Gil Savery, retired managing editor of the *Lincoln Journal*. After the war Eden and her husband, Winifield "Bud" Eden, ran a photography business in Lincoln until his death in 1979. Mae Eden then moved to Omaha, where she was active in community theater, before finally settling in Connecticut, where she died in 1996.

BONNIE REITAN AND THE NORTH PLATTE CANTEEN

During World War II the thousands of service members crossing the nation on Union Pacific trains always anticipated their brief stop in North Platte because they had heard of the warm welcome and homemade goodies awaiting them there. They would dash from their trains to the canteen that local volunteers like *North Platte Telegraph* reporter Bonnie Reitan helped staff at all hours of the day and night throughout the war. Two generations later canteen visitors told journalists and TV-documentary producers how vividly they recall getting a cake on their birthday or just a friendly greeting from the women who staffed the center. Noted Chicago journalist Bob Greene's book *Once Upon a Town* is a moving account of the enterprise. Although his account features canteen leaders, Reitan exemplifies the many North Platte women whose efforts made the project possible.

Reitan had joined the *Telegraph* in 1928, six months after graduating from high school in North Platte, for a starting salary of only ten dollars a week, but she loved the paper and spent twenty years as society editor and general reporter. "I did all of the society, I had the local page, I did obituaries, I did conventions, I did everything and counted out the papers to the paper boys. I went to work about 7:30 or 8 and if the paper was late I worked until 7 or 7:30 at night. And then in a month I got a raise to $10.50 a week. And then I worked there for 20 years and until Bill and I was married, the most I ever made was $23.20 take-home pay." When Bill joined the military, Reitan, who covered the canteen for the paper, joined a war-wives club whose members volunteered there. "There were 12 of us gals whose husbands were in the service. . . . If they [the canteen] had anybody in the evening and needed help, we girls would go down and take the baskets out to the fellas," she recalled years later. Workers carried baskets of food to soldiers on trains who could not come into the depot, a task that Reitan found "interesting." After the war Reitan left the paper but continued volunteering throughout North Platte. She started the Goodfellow Shoe Fund to help poor children and was active in everything from church to the American Legion Auxiliary until she died in 2003.

The young women who had found exciting careers in news during the war faced a postwar world that wanted them to return them to their prewar roles. Sometimes Rosie the Reporter married G.I. Joe and devoted herself to community volunteer work like Reitan, while others joined their husbands in a family business like Eden or accepted a traditional society news job like Paxson. In journalism as in so many fields, these traditionally female jobs paid less than comparable traditionally male jobs, as a 1946 *Lincoln Journal* pay scale demonstrates. "Society assistants" were grouped with secretarial help in a unit that started at $21.10 per week and topped out at $33 per week after four years while sports writers, reporters, and photographers were in a unit that started at $26.40 per week and rose to $56.10 per week after four years. A few women ventured into broadcasting although it still remained a predominantly male field, especially news casting. One of these pioneers was Betty Craig, last seen as a student reporter for UP's all-women wartime Lincoln bureau. Another was Martha Bohlsen, who became a major regional radio and TV personality for her long-running cooking show.

PIONEER WOMEN IN BROADCASTING

Craig spent several years with UP, learning a great deal under the demanding tutelage of Marguerite Davis, who often made her rewrite stories despite the tight wire-service deadlines and competition with AP. Davis insisted that Craig learn to do things right. In the late 1940s Craig joined KLIN in Lincoln as news director and also hosted an interview program featuring celebrities visiting Lincoln such as Senator Joseph McCarthy of Wisconsin, who had launched his controversial crusade against communism. Craig covered several of his visits to Nebraska but ran into difficulty when he spoke to an Omaha group that did not admit women, even women reporters. After McCarthy threatened to cancel the speech if Craig was barred, she was permitted to cover it.

In 1952 Craig joined the U.S. Senate staff of Fred Seaton of Hastings and worked for both Seaton and the Republican National Committee during the Eisenhower campaign that year. Later she returned to Lincoln as a trailblazing legislative reporter and staff member under the name of Betty Person; later still she became Betty Warner, wife of Jerome Warner of Waverly, one of Nebraska's most distinguished state senators.

While Craig's early work in broadcasting was nontraditional, another pioneer, Martha Bohlsen, built a large public following with her cooking shows. Bohlsen of Omaha's wow-TV was Nebraska's most famous woman broadcaster during the early years of TV. For a generation of homemakers in Nebraska and nine other midwestern states, she was like a daily friendly visitor offering advice on cooking and other homemaking concerns via radio and TV. By the end of her thirty-year broadcasting career, she was acclaimed as a pioneer in home economics programming and had received numerous national and local awards. In honor of her first twenty-five years in broadcasting, Mayor James Dworak proclaimed June 5, 1963, Martha Bohlsen Day in Omaha. She remained lifelong friends with her former wow-TV colleague Johnny Carson, later host of the *Tonight Show* on NBC.

Bohlsen grew up in Wausa, Nebraska, and took post–high school night classes in speech, nutrition, and food chemistry. She started her career as food editor of the old *Omaha Bee-News*, writing columns under the byline of Prudence Penny. She began a weekly radio show on home economics for the Electric Utilities in Omaha that was broadcast on virtually all Omaha radio stations and pioneered a new form of radio programming. In 1949 she joined the staff of wow radio and wow-TV just as wow-TV was going on the air. Here she did live daily radio and TV home economics shows, mostly on cooking. In a documentary about the early years of Omaha TV, she joked that viewers enjoyed her mistakes because they could identify with her. Bohlsen's audience expanded after she joined the Tidy House Products Company in 1953 as director of its Tidy House Kitchen Club. Her syndicated *Martha Bohlsen Show* was carried on sixty-nine radio stations and sixty-four TV stations in Nebraska, Iowa, North and South Dakota, Kansas, Minnesota, Illinois, Oklahoma, Colorado, and Wyoming. Whenever she offered a special bulletin with a collection of menus such as "Going to Church Dinners," more than five thousand viewers would respond by sending in their stamped, self-addressed envelopes to get the materials. Subscriptions to her Monthly Program Service summarizing her recipes and household hints came from forty-two states and some foreign countries. "Martha Bohlsen needs no introduction . . . because Martha is the undisputed owner of the title 'The Midwest's Most Popular Homemaker,'" wrote Omaha radio station KMEO in its spring 1963 publication. Her numerous honors include two McCalls awards. She died suddenly in 1984 and was elected to the Nebraska Broadcasting Hall of Fame in 1986.

WEEKLY EDITORS BUILD THEIR TOWNS

During the war Nebraska's economy recovered, and the last half of the decade was one of the most prosperous periods in the state's history. Small towns that had spent no money on infrastructure during the Depression and the war invested in hospitals, schools, streets, and parks, usually with the support of their local weekly newspapers. While many weekly editors headed major organizations, Ruth Best Pagel, editor of the *Neligh Leader*, made a difference through reporting that told the town of 1,700 about the benefits that the improvements would bring. The story of Pagel's accomplishments comes from interviews with her son, Alfred "Bud" Pagel, a retired journalism professor at the University of Nebraska–Lincoln, and her longtime competitor and admirer Emil Reutzel, who ran a weekly in Neligh and was managing editor of the *Norfolk Daily News*.

In his letter nominating Ruth Pagel for the Nebraska Press Association Hall of Fame, Reutzel described her as follows: "[She is] a well-liked lady who knows about everything — and I do mean everything — that is going on in town, or will be going on tomorrow and next week." Also Pagel could "turn out stories faster than Walter Winchell used to talk" and was "on a first name basis with everyone in the county." Reutzel praised his competitor and friend for her "thorough coverage" and her "special knack for being able to get the stories and beat the competition, fairly." And writing excellent copy was only part of what she did at the paper. She also worked with her husband, Alfred Sr., on advertising, bill collecting, bookkeeping, and production.

Ruth Pagel was born into a Neligh newspaper family although she spent much of her youth elsewhere. She succeeded her father, C. J. Best, as editor of the *Leader* after his death in 1941. Before becoming editor, however, she collected bills for the paper and did some writing plus caring for her children, Alfred Jr. and Shirley, and chairing the county Republican committee. Alfred Sr. was already the business manager when his wife became editor. Bud Pagel retains a vivid image of his mother sitting at her desk facing the front door and talking to all the people who came into the paper's office on Main Street. "She was very friendly; people just talked to her. She advised me that you want to be nice to everyone because you don't know when someone will be your next best source." Alfred Sr. told visitors to talk to Ruth because she was the editor.

The Neligh that Pagel covered had suffered badly during the drought and the Depression. Reutzel, who grew up there during the 1930s, recalled that the local hospital was a "few rooms in Dr. Harrison's home," and Main Street was the only paved road in town. The schools were old, but until the end of World War II, nothing changed except for the rebuilding of a pharmacy that burned in 1944. The town was ripe for change at the end of the war, and both local papers favored change although their advocacy took different forms. Reutzel was a civic leader and supported improvements through editorial statements. Pagel, however, believed in making her impact by fully and fairly covering all sides of stories rather editorializing. Her son said his mother was "real proud" that "because of her efforts there was a new school, hospital and swimming pool. She could itemize things that the paper had pushed" through its coverage of issues and problems.

Reutzel noted that in addition to being barred from important civic groups like Rotary and the American Legion because of her sex and lack of military service, Pagel was busy raising her children. Her life illustrated the juggling act that women editors had to perform and her own special sensitivity to people. Not only was she a great editor, but Bud's friends called her the "frog leg queen of Antelope County" because whenever they went frog hunting, she would cook their prey at all hours. One group she did lead was the Library Board, where she demonstrated the commonsense approach to problems that made her a successful editor. Once when some people complained that kids were ruining the grass by playing on a nearby swing, Ruth ruled in favor of the kids. They would grow up, and the grass would come back.

Pagel received several top weekly newspaper awards during her tenure and remained editor of her paper until 1963, when the family sold it to Reutzel. Bud Pagel, one of UNL's most beloved journalism instructors in modern times, said his mother's legacy lives on in the lessons she taught him, which he has passed on to his numerous journalism students. Ruth and Bud Pagel are the only mother and son in the Nebraska Press Association Hall of Fame.

COVERING THE WAR YEARS AND BEYOND

Within a week of Pearl Harbor, Nebraska's society sections had gone to war and remained on that footing for the duration, according to a sampling of *Omaha World-Herald* and *Lincoln Journal* editions.

Although the December 7, 1941, attack on Pearl Harbor immediately transformed the news sections of both newspapers, the transition to war footing was more gradual in both society sections. Both continued to report on holiday visitors and parties as well as weddings and engagements, club news, and other standard fare. One week after the Pearl Harbor attack, the *World-Herald* society section's lead story was headlined: "The 'Go' Signal Is On for Christmas Parties," but the lead tied the socializing to the war effort. "The 'go' signal is on for Christmas parties which, since the war began, have taken on added significance as a part of the 'keep the home fires burning' program for the home front." The page had a military flavor as another story reported on an army officers' wives luncheon at Fort Omaha where guests either sewed for the Red Cross or played bridge.

News sections in both papers reported on a wide range of women's contributions to the war effort, including the song that ninety-year-old Julia Bull of Omaha wrote predicting Japan's defeat. The photo page of that same edition featured a panel of fashions from previous wars and speculated that by 1943 women might be wearing "abbreviated trousers" that resemble today's capri pants. Men even got into social writing. Bill Billotte, who later became a *World-Herald* war correspondent, wrote a December 16, 1941, story about a Christmas party for the Thirty-Fifth Division.

By 1944 war dominated most news coverage, and society sections in both the Lincoln and the Omaha papers reflected this. Both printed large numbers of weddings and engagements, including some of military women whose engagement photos showed them in uniform. Both papers carried columns of news of local servicemen and women. Food columns in both papers featured recipes that could be made without sugar since it was rationed, and Red Cross news was prominent in the society and news sections of both papers. Both papers also featured stories on D-Day of the reaction at local canteens for servicemen as well as articles on war-loan drives, often pushed by women. War's end saw numerous stories in both papers welcoming returning veterans home, including women. On January 6, 1946, a story about women choosing hairdos to please returning G.I.s made the *World-Herald* news section. The January 6, 1946, *Lincoln Sunday Journal* and *Star* feature section displayed a large article headlined "War Agencies Demobilization," dealing mostly with the closing of a canteen for service members and recreation facilities such as an officers' lounge at the YMCA.

The news sections during the first week of January in 1946 and 1948 in both papers focused mainly on economic news and strikes. Social sections in both papers seemed shorter than in previous eras, sometimes occupying less than a full page on week days. There seemed to be fewer features about women in both news sections than during the war, and traditional food, fashion, and club news with copious stories about brides dominated the social sections. The numerous stories about brides were a harbinger of life in the upcoming 1950s, when most women, including some who would have outstanding journalistic careers, married young and usually deferred their own ambitions for the good of their families.

The change in tone from the way the papers covered women during World War I is impressive. While the newspapers' support for the war effort is obvious, the hard-edged propaganda tone of World War I is absent. After Pearl Harbor there was no need to persuade the nation about the reasons for going to war. The treatment of women had also improved greatly since World War I. Women were now portrayed as respected adults making important contributions to the war effort both in and out of uniform, not as "girls" regardless of their age. Although I examined a lot of World War II microfilm, I never saw a cutesy story about women and the military, and the language feminizing every position (sailorette) is long gone. One finds numerous pictures of women in uniform and serious discussions about the impact of the war on family life throughout the papers. Women may still have occupied a relatively separate sphere, but it was a much larger sphere that overlapped significantly with the men's sphere. The women who filled it were viewed as adults making important contributions to the war effort, not as fragile creatures who must be chaperoned and sheltered like their counterparts during World War I. The "Rosies" who filled formerly male roles throughout society, including those in journalism, did indeed lay the groundwork for the changes that their daughters would experience a generation later. Their contributions deserve our recognition, but the postwar fate of women should serve as a reminder that breakthroughs can be reversed, at least temporarily.

7 | The 1950s

During the 1950s Nebraskans were both prosperous and perennially frightened. They watched *Leave It to Beaver* on TV, but their children practiced hiding under school desks during air-raid drills, and they watched missile silos being dug in cornfields to counter the threat of a Soviet attack. Residents felt the Soviet menace every time the cold war heated up because Strategic Air Command Headquarters at Offutt Air Force Base was a prime target, and network documentaries depicting the devastation of a nuclear strike sometimes used Omaha as their example. Daily life played out against this chilling backdrop as couples married and had children young; joined churches, PTAs, and bowling leagues; and shot fireworks on the Fourth of July. Women, who subordinated their ambitions to those of their husbands, devoted themselves to raising the baby boomers, gardening, canning, and sewing to stretch the family budget for summer vacations to the Black Hills or even Disneyland or luxuries like window air conditioners. Families sampled the TV dinners invented in Omaha as they watched situation comedies and westerns together, and parents hoped that Elvis would not be a bad influence on their teens. By the end of the decade, the first Valentino's Pizza had opened in Lincoln, and suburban shopping centers would soon challenge the primacy of shopping in downtown Omaha as more and more residents moved to the western edge of the city. In 1958 Charles Starkweather's murderous rampage terrified residents and gave Nebraska unwanted national notoriety.

For women journalists nationally and locally, the 1950s were generally a time of limited opportunities. "Newspapers rarely hired women. When they did it was to work on the women's section," wrote historian Kay Mills. "The same kind of women who had been welcomed at the city desk in wartime couldn't get past the front desk." Occasionally employers made an exception for an "exceptional woman," but most believed that "the newsroom was no place for a lady." However, Nebraska produced several noted women journalists during the decade: NU alum Marianne Hansen Means became a Washington correspondent for Hearst Newspapers and was assigned to the Kennedy campaign and the White House. Betty Craig Person Warner covered state government for the *Lincoln Star*. The first women broke into TV reporting in Omaha, and three Nebraska women reporters broke ground by covering the Starkweather case. Glaring inequalities remained, especially in Omaha, where there were no women TV anchors, and the *Omaha World-Herald* had no women city news reporters. However, in the days before equal employment opportunity legislation, no one questioned this situation because that's just how things were. The double standard began in college, where women recall equal treatment in the classroom but restrictions outside it that men did not face.

A female journalism major at the University of Nebraska in the 1950s could boss male colleagues as editor of the *Daily Nebraskan*, but if news broke after her 10:00 p.m. weeknight curfew, she would be confined to her campus residence while they covered the action. For example, when panty raiders invaded female residences during the early fifties causing considerable damage, *Daily Nebraskan* editor Joan Krueger, a future president of the University of Alaska, was forced to remain in the Gamma Phi Beta sorority house while her associate, Don Pieper, roamed the campus covering the outbreak. Authorities allowed a few exceptions to the curfew rules. Ruth Raymond Thone, a *Daily Nebraskan* editor who would later juggle her writing career with life as a political wife, recalled that the dean of women permitted women night news editors to work late at the *Lincoln Star* checking the next day's edition, but the dean worried about exposing women to the foul language that she assumed printers used, even though this had never been a problem.

Journalism professors treated women as equals in class, but Beverly Buck Pollock, who later published the *Keith County News* with her husband, Jack, recalls challenging a professor who complimented her for thinking like a man. "I went walking down the hall with him and said, 'What did you say?' He quickly said, 'You think like a very intelligent human being.'" Most women married soon after graduating and subordinated their ambitions to the needs of their husbands and children. News organizations usually hired them for lower-level jobs than their male classmates. Thone, for example, initially typed editorials for the *Lincoln Star's* chief editorial writer Jimmy Lawrence, even though she had previously covered the courthouse and "absolutely everything" else for her hometown *Scottsbluff Star-Herald*. Within six months the *Star* promoted her to reporter, and years later she said, "I was never aware of any prejudice against women in journalism." Thone left the newspaper to marry her husband, Charles, a lawyer who was elected to Congress, then became governor of Nebraska, but she never abandoned journalism. She wrote columns for the *Lincoln Star* and the *Omaha World-Herald*, contributed freelance articles to the *Washington Post*, and wrote commentary for Nebraska public radio. She also has written several books about women.

Journalism was one of a handful of occupations that offered an alternative to the standard careers then open to women: teaching, nursing, and office work. Janet Stefan Pieper, a math major who worked on the *Daily Nebraskan*, interned at the *Norfolk Daily News* and felt lucky to do so: "While my friends were plucking chickens. I got to proofread and write and walked the streets looking for news." Women journalism majors struck Pieper as "more worldly somehow and more career-oriented" than most other women students. However, when they graduated, "most of the women started as clerks or death and weather writers. . . . I am pretty sure that men had better job opportunities right out of college." Pieper, who eventually earned a doctorate and served as a cabinet member under Governor Thone, taught wherever her husband Don Pieper's career took them. When Don took a job with UPI in Omaha, she enrolled in a master's program in English at Omaha University and taught English there, but she was forced to quit when she became pregnant. "The president called me into his office and said I could finish the first semester, but I was starting to 'show' and that was not appropriate. That is a story today's women find difficult to believe." Later she wrote a Lincoln "society column" for the *Omaha World-Herald* after her editor agreed to let her write "about interesting women doing meaningful things." However, after Pieper quit, the column "became more social again."

Pollock, whose family published the *Nebraska Farmer* and other magazines, married her husband, Jack, shortly after both graduated from the University of Nebraska in 1958. He became news editor of the *Sidney Telegraph*, and she became a reporter there. After several years they moved to Ogallala and purchased the *Keith County News*, their joint career venture for life. Although Pollock grew up in Lincoln, she had always spent her summers on a family ranch in the Sand Hills and loved western Nebraska. As copublisher of the *Keith County News*, she wrote an award-winning column and "did anyone's job that needed to be done." One winter when Jack was sailing in the Caribbean with some friends, leaving Bev in command, the weather turned awful and the pipes froze. Then the sports editor's mother died, and the lifestyle editor fell ill. "The news editor and I wrote the whole paper," she recalled. When Jack arrived home, Bev greeted him with a "For Sale" sign in their yard! In 2002 Pollock won the National Newspaper Association's Emma C. McKinley Memorial Award, the top honor for a woman in community journalism. In her acceptance speech, she said: "My husband and I have worked as a team — a team of community journalists — and I can't imagine a better or more rewarding career." In 2011 Pollock became a charter member of the Nebraska Press Women's Hall of Fame.

Although Thone, Pieper, and Pollock became successful despite marrying young and integrating their careers with the demands of family, a few women defied the decade's norms from the start. These included retired Hearst syndicated columnist Marianne Means, a 1956 University of Nebraska graduate from Sioux City, Iowa, who began her Washington reporting career after a few years of working on smaller papers. Her path to fame began at the university when Senator John F. Kennedy and his speechwriter Theodore C. Sorensen, a Nebraska alum whose sister belonged to Means's sorority, visited campus.

MAKING IT IN WASHINGTON DC

Means, who had worked hard to persuade Kennedy to come to NU, escorted the two around campus and reconnected with Sorensen and JFK a few years later when Hearst Newspapers assigned her to cover Kennedy's presidential campaign. In her 2008 retirement column, Means wrote that she didn't remember much about Kennedy's fateful visit "except that Sorensen growled to Kennedy, 'Presidential candidates don't chew gum' as [they] approached the speech site. Out went the gum."

Means moved to Washington during the Eisenhower administration and found her first presidential press conference representing Hearst Newspapers a memorable experience. "President Dwight D. Eisenhower failed to recognize my wildly flailing arm and call on me although I was the only woman in the press contingent (or maybe because I was). If I had worn a red dress it probably wouldn't have helped."

In Washington Means applied for radio jobs, but men repeatedly told her, "Nobody will take a woman's voice seriously." Hearst assigned her to cover the Kennedy campaign because "the bu-

reau was very short-staffed at the time and [her] salary was pea-
nuts." The Hearst organization was also aware of her Nebraska
ties to Sorensen, Kennedy's closest aide. "When Kennedy actually won the election, the startled Hearst bureau looked around
and decided to take a chance on a young woman who could write
and who knew some of Kennedy's aides and the president himself." She was in the lead press bus in Dallas when Kennedy was
shot and covered the "traumatic events that followed." Means
also covered Kennedy's successor, President Lyndon Johnson,
whom she called "magnificent" in pushing civil rights and other
legislation through Congress. Unfortunately "all of his good
works have been submerged in the Vietnam disaster." In 1965 she
left reporting to become a syndicated columnist for the next forty
years. She also wrote a book (*The Women in the White House*)
and received numerous awards, including election to member-
ship in the Sigma Delta Chi (journalism professional honorary)
Hall of Fame. In her final column she reflected on the changing
media world. "In the old days when I was younger, we liked stories about perfect lives and hairdos — we wanted to believe. They
were in charge! And now we've become much more skeptical and
hopefully, realistic. . . . And the media are very confused. . . . It's
a new world for someone else to figure out. . . . But hang on — I
may be back."

COVERING NEBRASKA STATE GOVERNMENT:
BETTY CRAIG PERSON WARNER

Means wasn't the only Nebraska woman journalist seeking success in Washington at the time. Betty Craig, pioneer KLIN news
director, joined the U.S. senator Fred Seaton's staff there in 1952.
After Eisenhower appointed Seaton secretary of the interior,
Craig moved to the Library of Congress, where she wrote a history of the U.S. capitol. She also married and divorced, then returned to Lincoln in 1956 as Betty Person and began covering
state government for the *Lincoln Star*. As the highly respected

Person became acquainted with state government, she realized that senators needed research help and suggested that they create such a position. In 1964 the legislature hired her as its only research staffer, a position she held until she retired in 1971 following her marriage the year before to the influential Senator Jerome Warner of Waverly. When she died in 1994, leaders of both parties praised her integrity and competence. "Betty Person — that was her name then — was one of the finest reporters I've ever known," said former governor Frank Morrison. "She was always well-informed on the subject matter she was covering and asked good questions. Every day she came in to interview me was a pleasure."

INEQUALITY IN OMAHA

Unlike the Lincoln papers, the *World-Herald* restricted women to social news during the 1950s, and Omaha TV stations were nearly all male. Talent and credentials made little difference as the case of future Living section editor Patricia Wolfe illustrates. In 1950 the *World-Herald* hired Wolfe as a secretary to managing editor Fred Ware, although she was an honors journalism graduate of the University of Iowa and previously had been a reporter-photographer at the *Davenport (IA) Times*. She accepted the secretarial job because "if you need a job you take a job." Wolfe said that many *World-Herald* men "really didn't think women belonged in city news," but "smaller papers were willing to take women."

When Wolfe moved to Women's News, her duties included calling prominent people "on the horrible calling list" seeking news about their activities. "I hated it as did most people." Only a few department staffers had professional journalism training, which hurt the section's reputation within the newsroom, although Wolfe was universally respected as a fine writer and one of the paper's best editors. However, changing times contributed to her ability to revolutionize Women's News when she became the department's editor in 1970. To upgrade the staff she hired excellent journalists with expertise in fields such as food writing then worked behind the scenes with top managers to persuade them it was time to convert women's news to a features section. Ironically Wolfe's supervisors initially resisted her proposals for change "because they enjoyed reading social news." By the time Wolfe retired in 1988, Women's News had been renamed Living, and the section focused on cultural and consumer news, changing lifestyles, and family problems in addition to carrying traditional social items. Wolfe was especially proud of the talented staff she had hired. "We had a wonderful staff of all college graduates." The *World-Herald* changes were consistent with national trends in women's news sections during that period.

BREAKING BARRIERS IN TELEVISION

Early broadcast news did not welcome women as Marianne Means and others discovered, but the door cracked open for two Omaha women during the 1950s. In 1952 Dorothy Hayes Sater joined wow radio and tv, covering stories, although she was classified officially as a secretary, something she did not realize during her newsroom tenure. Five years later Ninette Beaver took a temporary part-time reporting job at kmtv that lasted for thirty-five years. Although she was never officially employed "full-time" (despite weeks that could total fifty or more hours), she gained national fame for her coverage of the Starkweather case and its aftermath. Both Sater and Beaver are recognized today as women pioneers in Omaha broadcast news despite Sater's official job classification and Beaver's "part-time" status. Their experiences illuminate what life was like for women in tv news at that time.

Sater was a journalism student at Omaha University when she joined wow radio and tv. She covered stories, took photos, wrote newscasts, and rewrote wire copy for on-air delivery, although like most reporters and photographers of the era, she turned her stories and pictures over to newscasters and never appeared on camera. "The only thing I did as a secretary was to answer the phones. I was in charge of our correspondents in Nebraska and Western Iowa. I would take their stories." A pay dispute led to her departure from WOW in 1959. She had asked for a raise, but station head Frank Fogarty refused and told her that he did not want women in his newsroom. Sater said that after Fogarty told her, "You should be home raising a family," she went back to the newsroom, concluded that "there wasn't much future" for her in broadcasting, and decided to leave. She took a job at Omaha University, and after several career, family, and location changes, she moved into hospital PR in Omaha, from which she later retired. Many consider her to be Omaha's first full-time woman TV reporter despite her official job classification. She died in 2012 just weeks before she would have received the Career Achievement Award from the Omaha Press Club Foundation.

Beaver, who still enjoys national recognition for her coverage of the Starkweather case, became a journalist almost accidentally when her neighbor in Council Bluffs, Iowa, who was a stringer for the *Des Moines Register* got sick and asked her to fill in. Beaver had studied sociology at Creighton University but married before graduating. She was staying home with her two children at the time and figured she might as well try reporting. Her assignments introduced her to the Omaha reporters who were covering stories in Council Bluffs, and when a KMTV reporter was drafted, the station hired her as a temporary replacement despite her gender. Popular newscaster Floyd Kalber told Beaver that he "had a policy against women in the newsroom," but she did such a good job that he extended her employment. Thus Beaver was in the newsroom when shocking news of mass murder in Lincoln broke. "I was in the right place at the right time."

For three days in January 1958, Charles Starkweather, age nineteen, of Lincoln terrorized Nebraska by killing eleven people. Caril Ann Fugate, fourteen, whose mother, stepfather, and step-sister were among the victims, accompanied him. Both Stark-weather and Fugate were convicted of first-degree murder. Stark-weather was electrocuted and Fugate sentenced to life in prison despite her youth and her protestations of innocence. Beaver and two Lincoln women reporters, Nancy Benjamin of the *Lincoln Star* and Marjorie Marlette of the *Lincoln Evening Journal*, helped cover the rampage and its aftermath, although it was rare for women to cover crime in the 1950s. All continued to write about the case for years.

After helping KMTV organize its initial coverage, Beaver went to Lincoln, where most of the action was occurring. She discov-ered where Starkweather's parents lived and paid them a surprise visit along with a photographer. The parents agreed to an on-camera interview after Beaver persuaded them that it was im-portant to speak for themselves; the interview also was the first time that she had appeared on camera. Beaver covered Stark-weather's trial and tried unsuccessfully to interview him. After his conviction she sought an interview with Fugate, but the teen's attorneys instead organized a press conference with twenty-five other reporters. Beaver finally talked with Fugate one-on-one as the jury was deliberating her fate, then was in court later that night when the jury announced her conviction. In the years that followed, Beaver did a number of stories on Fugate, notably her 1972 NBC News documentary "Growing Up in Prison," which re-broadcast original footage from the case and followed Fugate's daily life in prison. The contrast between the hostile teenager of 1958 and the poised adult prisoner helped build public support for Fugate's parole. Beaver also coauthored *Caril*, recounting the Starkweather-Fugate cases and Fugate's life in prison. Eventually Fugate was released, and Beaver has since retired.

At the *Lincoln Star* Nancy Benjamin urged city editor Earl Dyer to send her into a neighborhood where people had been killed. He refused because Starkweather was still at large and many Lin-colnites were armed, but years later he praised her eagerness to cover the story. In a memoir of covering Starkweather, Dyer wrote, "Nancy Benjamin, always a feisty and ambitious reporter, wanted to go to the Ward neighborhood and ring doorbells to get neighbors' reactions and any facts they might know. But with his mind on the number of weapons being sold in gun stores and being displayed on the streets, Dyer ordered her to stay in the office — telephoning interviews with the neighbors might be less impressive in the next morning's paper but it would be safer." Benjamin wrote a six-part series on what prompted Starkweather's rampage and asked whether anything could have been done to prevent it. She continued to write about the case until she moved to San Diego. The *Lincoln Evening Journal*'s Marjorie Marlette, a pioneer woman courts and corrections reporter, also became noted for her work on the Starkweather and Fugate cases. In an early profile of Starkweather, she "sounded a note to be repeated many times — that the young man had shown no advance sign that he could become a mass killer." She not only helped cover his trial but provided Starkweather with the legal forms for his appeal. Marlette also covered Fugate's appeals, including the 1976 hearing where she finally won parole. In 1982 Governor Thone appointed Marlette to the state parole board. She died in 1999. She was elected to the Nebraska Press Women's Hall of Fame as a charter member in 2011.

BUSINESS AS USUAL IN WOMEN'S NEWS

Rather than randomly spot-check editions of the *World-Herald* for social news, I decided that examining the two weeks encompassing the Starkweather murders might offer a good indication of its status during this era. Since 1958 was a fairly typical year except for the case, the two weeks provided a good window into the paper as a whole before the shocking crimes began. Surprisingly, women's news did not resemble the women's magazines that I remember reading during these years (I was in grade school and read everything available that did not involve farming or mechanics). The biggest surprise was that it was difficult to even *find* the women's news section except on Sundays and Fridays (food day). Daily papers carried just a few columns of social notes that weren't even labeled as a section. This was more surprising because the decade stressed family togetherness and domesticity, surely a time when women whose primary occupation was homemaking could have expected the paper to provide lots of information on childrearing, food preparation, and fashion. As nearly as I could tell, the daily paper offered only modest amounts of such information.

Here is a sample of what a *World-Herald* reader would have found in 1958 in the paper as a whole. On Sunday, January 26, two days before the murders began, the page 1 lead headline was "Russia Favors ICBM Talks on Own Terms." The Midlands news section led with a political article, "Donald Ross Seems Ahead for GOP Job." In sports, the Golden Gloves boxing tournament led the section, while women's news featured a story on tobogganing. The section contained numerous stories about weddings and engagements, Mary Lane's local advice column, social items from outside Omaha, and a food story, "Fluff Dessert Uses Leftover Cake." On Monday, January 27, the cold war again dominated the front page with two frightening stories: "Vanguard Launching Fizzles Again" and "Russia Stalls Peace Talks." There were no stories of consequence in women's news. For the rest of the week, Starkweather dominated page 1 as the death toll climbed from three to ten. On Thursday, January 30, an eight-column headline across the front page screamed "Punk's Blood-Stained String Ends at 10 with Wyoming Capture." The final body was discovered later. Throughout this period, the paper contained several columns of social news with no apparent reflection of the dramatic local events unfolding. By Sunday, February 2, life had returned more or less to normal. The front page of the Midlands news section discussed the reluctance of girls to talk about politics, while women's news featured Mardi Gras plans at Duchesne, a Catholic high school and college for women. Readers interested in the accomplishments of women could find occasional stories in the news section such as a February 3 article reporting that Joanna Nelle had been named editor of the *Creightonian*, Creighton University's student newspaper.

It is interesting that the newspapers of the 1950s offered the fewest insights into the daily lives of women of any decade examined. Given the high value that the 1950s placed on women in the home and the general affluence of the period, it seems amazing that advertising targeting women shoppers did not generate more news aimed specifically at them. The food section, which was tied to the highly lucrative weekly grocery ads, is extensive but differs greatly from the food coverage of today. It consisted almost entirely of recipes with little or no mention of nutrition, let alone the merits of organic versus nonorganic products and similar topics. In this sense it reflects a decade when homemakers took pride in being able to afford to buy their bread rather than bake it and cooking with canned soup and other packaged products such as gelatin was fashionable. It is still surprising how little space the newspaper allocated to women's news, especially in the daily editions. Perhaps this alone is an indication of the extent to which women were marginalized during the period, a situation that would change drastically with the coming of the 1960s and 1970s, when all those baby boomers came of age and began demanding opportunities commensurate with their education. These demands would reshape life for women in all fields, including journalism, locally and nationally.

8 | The 1960s

When John F. Kennedy offered the nation a New Frontier during the 1960 presidential campaign, Nebraskans responded by giving his opponent, Richard Nixon, the highest percentage vote of any state. The "new frontier" that they welcomed was the beginning of Coach Bob Devaney's Cornhusker dynasty, which became one of the few bright spots for traditionalists in the tumultuous decade. Kennedy's top aide Theodore Sorensen infuriated many of his fellow Nebraskans when he made a speech in 1961 calling his home state "old, outmoded, a place to come from or a place to die." Residents protested but sensed that he might be right as educated young people left for states with more exciting lifestyles and better economic opportunities. Even those who stayed in Nebraska settled in Lincoln and Omaha far more often than they returned to small towns.

The student revolution never caught on in Nebraska as it did in more liberal states with higher percentages of young people. In the late 1960s there was a small Students for a Democratic Society (SDS) chapter at the University of Nebraska, but it was more of a curiosity than a threat to the establishment. By contrast the Greek system flourished, and the young people selling flowers on Lincoln street corners on football Saturdays were members of pep organizations, not hippies. Today's college students can hardly believe there was a time when women could not wear jeans or shorts to class or dinner and that they could be "campused" for infractions like staying out too late, failing to draw their curtains after sunset, or failing to sign out whenever they left their residences. However, university administrators did not need to worry about their offices being occupied because students preferred to negotiate for an end to "in loco parentis," curfews for women, and dress codes rather confront authority figures. The University of Nebraska was "with it" enough to draw a visit from the beat poet Allen Ginsberg but traditional enough that the visit provoked controversy. By the late 1960s more women were seeking better opportunities as larger numbers applied to law, medical, and graduate school, a rarity earlier in the decade. In 1967, for example, only two women graduated from the University of Nebraska College of Medicine, and there were no women in any of the photos of the College of Law in the Cornhusker yearbook. A few more women studied journalism as an alternative to teaching or landing in the typing pool after graduation, but sex discrimination remained pervasive.

By the end of the 1960s, the Vietnam War dominated the headlines as fighting intensified and college graduates faced being drafted to fight a war that few any longer believed in. As the death toll in Vietnam rose with seemingly no end in sight, Nebraskans grew more troubled about it. By the early 1970s there was considerable antiwar sentiment at some of the state's colleges, but except for the brief student occupation of NU's Military and Naval Science Building following President Nixon's 1970 invasion of Cambodia, protests were peaceful. In 1968 Nebraska briefly reached national headlines as senators Robert F. Kennedy and Eugene McCarthy contested the Democratic presidential primary a month before Kennedy's assassination. Kennedy, who resonated with alienated groups, developed a surprising affinity for the state during his campaign, according to historian Arthur Schlesinger. "He [Kennedy] liked Nebraska, said [astronaut] John Glenn. 'The plain physical beauty of the countryside and the square fields and the plow patterns,' and the greenness of the Midwestern spring. And he liked the farmers. 'He really felt,' said [aide] Peter Edelman, 'that they, in a romantic kind of way . . . were his kind of people.' He had found 'another kind of forgotten and alienated

American, another person who thought that this system had just left him behind.'"

When the 1960s began, sex discrimination in employment was legal and widespread. By the end of the decade, it was illegal and still widespread, but an assertive new generation was challenging the status quo. These women had grown up watching the civil rights struggle on TV and had helped eliminate college rules restricting women. They were comfortable challenging tradition and assumed that they had a right to any careers they chose. Now they *would* open journalism fully to women, not only for themselves but for their future daughters. The idealists among them saw journalism as a way to make the world better, making this a selfless fight for justice consistent with their traditional midwestern feminine values such as concern for others more than self. These women understood that to succeed, they had to excel on tough assignments without seeming so tough that they alienated male colleagues, whose good will they needed long term. They had to grit their teeth at sexist humor and prove their steeliness while remaining feminine. Some compared it to walking an invisible tightrope. No one performed the act of balancing journalistic toughness with traditional Nebraska feminine niceness better than Beverly Deepe of Belvidere, a top war correspondent in Vietnam from 1962 to 1969. But she was far from alone as numerous Nebraska women during these years quietly broke down sexual barriers in all fields of journalism locally; several, including Lynne Grasz and Trudy Lieberman, launched nationally important careers that continue into the present. Omaha lagged behind Lincoln in opening major media jobs to women, but even there a few women were beginning to break down traditional barriers.

BEVERLY DEEPE: COVERING VIETNAM

The day after South Vietnamese president Diem was assassinated in 1963, *Newsweek* correspondent Beverly Deepe entered his palace through a hole in the six-inch-thick wall to give her readers a sense of the "unbelievable" disorder in the family quarters, including things like scattered men's magazines and Madame Nhu's pink bathrobes. While Deepe was inspecting the palace, Diem's troops looted her apartment half a block from the palace and sprayed it with gunfire, possibly in retaliation for her coverage of the Buddhist protests against Diem's regime. When Deepe, the first woman war correspondent in Vietnam, arrived in Saigon in 1962, a male colleague dismissed her as a "sweet, corn-fed, innocent girl." By the time she left seven years later, her final employer there, the *Christian Science Monitor*, nominated her for a Pulitzer Prize for a series evaluating whether the results of the war justified its costs. Unlike reporters who cycled in and out of Vietnam, Deepe lived in Saigon and reported for a succession of major publications, including the *London Daily* and the *Sunday Express* and the *New York Herald Tribune* in addition to *Newsweek* and the *Christian Science Monitor*. She focused on her work even when male colleagues called her a "boring, farm-bred Nebraska girl." During her seven years in Vietnam, Deepe covered the Tet Offensive and other major battles as well as well as writing numerous articles on Vietnam's politics, economics, and culture.

Deepe always valued her rural Nebraska roots. "Growing up on the farm showed me the need for hard work, the discipline to perform that work when it needed to be done, the unpredictability of nature, and the rewards of taking well-calculated risks." She had dreamed of seeing how people in other parts of the world lived ever since reading Pearl Buck's novel about China, *The Good Earth*, while she was a child at the Coon Ridge country school near Belvidere in southern Nebraska. The school lacked amenities such as indoor plumbing and electricity, but it fed a bright girl's imagination and travel lust. After winning a writing award in high school, she double majored in journalism and political science at the University of Nebraska, where the French she studied to cover Paris fashion shows eventually helped her get her job at *Newsweek* in Vietnam. Deepe graduated Phi Beta Kappa in 1957, interned for the Associated Press in Des Moines, and enrolled in the Columbia University Graduate School of Journalism, from which she also graduated with honors. She credits William F. Hall, head of NU's journalism school, for much of her professional success. "He arrived in about my junior year, as I recall, and was a ball of fire. . . . He somehow arranged for me to get that summer job with the Associated Press in Des Moines, which he said I needed for some professional experience so as to get me into the Columbia Graduate School of Journalism in New York. . . . I'm sure his recommendation was key to my being admitted because the class I joined was so superb."

In 1961 Deepe began a trip around the world but could not disembark in Shanghai to realize her dream of seeing China because it was closed to Americans. However, in Hong Kong AP bureau chief Roy Essoyan urged her to visit Saigon because "things [were] really heating up in Vietnam." She abandoned the rest of her trip and settled in Saigon.

> During my seven years of reporting there, I traveled by military helicopter, airplane, jeep and riverboat, pedicabs and taxi to report on the two-track war of insurgency and infiltration. I even rode an elephant in the jungle highlands in the early years before these elegant beasts were destroyed by the bombing and the fighting. . . . I experimented with doing [Columbia professor Samuel] Lubell-styled talks with rice-paddy families about their lives, visited old west styled border forts that became overrun or abandoned before I departed the country, and interviewed many sources ranging from Vietnamese fighters on both sides, American advisers and later U.S. combat soldiers, coup-makers and plotters, distraught Buddhist bonzes, and even fortune-tellers. I agonized with the dead, the wounded and the homeless. It was hectic, hellish journalism and almost-instant, ultimately heartbreaking history.

Even though Deepe broke professional barriers as the permanent female member of the Saigon press corps, according to historian Joyce Hoffmann, she "held a remarkably orthodox view of her role in a war zone. . . . Although she doubtless wanted the same freedoms and opportunities for which her feminist sisters would soon begin marching in America, Deepe clung to what she perceived as society's expectations for women: 'I should be feminine, but not fragile; change from sport dress to flight suit as most women change from slacks to skirt; look fresh in fatigues during a downpour or scaling a slippery rice dike,' she explained. . . . 'It's more important to wear lipstick than a pistol.'" After leaving Vietnam, Deepe married Lt. Col. Charles Keever, a Marine whom she met when he was assigned to escort her in combat. She taught journalism and received numerous freedom-of-information awards during her twenty-nine years at the University of Hawai'i, from which she retired in 2008.

EDUCATING BOOMER WOMEN JOURNALISTS

While Deepe was settling into Saigon, the first baby boomers were entering college and discovering that their professors included a few groundbreaking women journalism faculty members such as Wilma Crumley at the University of Nebraska and Mary Williamson at Omaha University. (Omaha University merged with the University of Nebraska to become the University of Nebraska at Omaha in 1968.) These professors sought to prepare their women students to conquer a field that still discriminated against them without unduly frightening them. "It was better for them to hit the world not expecting discrimination, but once it touched you, to be prepared to do everything you were capable of," said Crumley. "It was important that our students did not have the perception that they were limited." As a pioneer in Nebraska newspaper advertising who was one of the first women to receive a doctorate in journalism from the University of Missouri, she knew what women might encounter.

Crumley, who died in 2009, instilled confidence by making demands and recognizing achievement. She was elected to the Nebraska Press Women's Hall of Fame in 2011. Williamson did the same for women at UNO. Women gained additional confidence by working on college newspapers and in radio stations, where they routinely held top jobs and enjoyed their camaraderie with male colleagues. Later they sought to replicate these experiences and relationships in professional newsrooms.

An unusual combination of social and economic conditions abetted the changes the boomers sought. The robust economy of the late 1960s required the skills of women knowledge workers; birth control became widespread, allowing women to delay pregnancy until their careers were established; and middle-class families increasingly required two incomes to afford their lifestyles so there were fewer debates about whether wives should work. This convergence of factors combined with the determination of the boomers to find their rightful places in the professional world reshaped both their lives and their country.

EXPANDING ROLES IN BROADCASTING

Broadcasting had always been a male field in which a few women found a place, but this was changing. In 1969 the Federal Communications Commission banned sex discrimination, opening the way for an influx of women. At small family-owned radio stations, progress had already begun. Georgia Crawford and her husband started KCNI in Broken Bow in 1949, and she served as general manager for over twenty-two years. In addition to writing commercials and doing the bookkeeping, she hosted the *Kitchen Kate* and *Local News and Views* weekday programs. In 1978 she was the first woman inducted into the Nebraska Broadcasters' Hall of Fame. At North Platte's KODY, Geraldine Wing rose from secretary to general manager during her long career. Her duties included bookkeeping, traffic, selling advertising, and "on air" work. Joan Wood entered broadcasting as a bookkeeper at KSID radio in Sidney in 1967 and eventually became general manager of KIMB in Kimball. In 1968 Ruth Williams became a copywriter at WOW-AM-FM-TV in Omaha and eventually was promoted to creative director. She became a member of the WOWT management team when the TV and radio operations separated in 1973.

The stereotype that viewers found women less authoritative than men was a barrier to women in broadcasting, especially TV, but during the late 1960s local stations started hiring attractive "weather girls" to raise ratings. Unfortunately some viewers mistakenly assumed that any attractive woman covering weather was a bimbo. However, Linda Dierking Beermann, the first woman in news at Lincoln's KOLN/KGIN-TV, demolished such myths by covering all types of stories and broadcasting the weather. Beermann, a Nebraska City native and Phi Beta Kappa journalism graduate of NU, had proved that she could handle the toughest assignments during her internship at KMTV when she drove around North Omaha during an outbreak of racial violence. "This was considered quite dangerous, but I never felt in personal danger." She interned at KMTV again after graduating, but since there was no fulltime opening, she accepted a fill-in job as street reporter and photographer at KOLN/KGIN-TV that lasted twenty years. Her assignments included the legislature, police, "and just about everything." One cold New Year's day, she accompanied officers looking for a decapitated murder victim's head. "I wasn't going to wimp out because I was a female."

Beermann became assignment editor in 1973 but is best remembered for doing weathercasts during the 1970s and 1980s, especially throughout her two pregnancies. A tall brunette, she was surprised when station manager A. James Ebel chose her to broadcast the weather instead of a "blonde pixie" because "he thought [she] came across better." She raised news-show ratings during one of her pregnancies as viewers tuned in to see if her child had arrived. She said that appearing on TV while visibly pregnant with her second child in 1985 upset some viewers, and a handful protested. Ironically there had been no protests during her first pregnancy in 1980 because the station had shot mostly head and shoulders views of her, but later technology required full views. Today she is a community volunteer in Lincoln.

Another KOLN/KGIN-TV pioneer was Leta Powell Drake, who hosted and produced more than ten thousand TV shows during her twenty-eight years with the station, the *10/11 Morning Show*, and *Cartoon Corral with Kalamity Kate*. In 1982 she became program director. She joined the staff of NETV in 1989 and programmed the Nebraska Public Television Network for the next thirteen years. In 2010 Drake was elected to the Nebraska Broadcasters Association Hall of Fame.

Broadcasting breakthroughs came not only in commercial television but in the state's important educational TV network, which offered parts of western Nebraska their only access to TV in the presatellite era. During the 1960s Janet Poley gave the network's *House and Home* show a contemporary vibe that stressed consumer education and protection, healthy lifestyles, nutrition, creative activities for children, family financial management, and services for people with disabilities. Poley, a Nebraska City native who had majored in home economics and broadcast journalism at NU, took viewers "on the road" to "nearly every museum and tourist attraction in the state," including the governor's mansion and Omaha's Old Market. She wrote and produced the show in addition to hosting it from 1965 to 1975, serving as both a senior producer at NETV and a faculty member in NU's Department of Agricultural Communication. "I had total responsibility for everything — even cleaning the mice off the set. In those days it was a rehearsal and straight through the live program," she said. Challenges included the program's lack of budget. "I either spent my own money, begged, or created things from nothing." She even enlisted her mother to make puppets for scene transitions. Educational TV stations in Iowa, Wisconsin, and other midwestern states picked up the program. That ended when Poley took a job in international development at the U.S. Department of Agriculture in Washington DC. She later ran a U.S. Agency for International Development program in Tanzania and became president and CEO of the American Distance Education Consortium while living in Lincoln.

ADVANCING IN NEWSPAPERS

Women had long covered hard news in Lincoln in contrast with their situation in Omaha, but during the 1960s their numbers and responsibilities expanded, partially fueled by the growing numbers of talented women graduating from NU's journalism school. Marjorie Marlette continued her groundbreaking coverage of prisons, and Bess Jenkins became health reporter for the *Lincoln Evening Journal*, while Cella Heitman (later Quinn) covered city hall and Rose Sipe was assistant city editor. Women including Cheryl Parks Butler, Jan Sack, and Jan Kreuscher joined the copy desk. Kreuscher, who left the paper when her former husband was drafted and returned when he was in law school, retains fond memories of the *Journal* despite her discovery that women were paid less than men. "I always felt that at the *Journal* you could do almost anything if you didn't demand to be paid for it." She unsuccessfully protested the unequal pay policy after accidentally seeing the pay stub of a male colleague who was being paid more although they had equivalent responsibilities. Her boss rejected her request for equal pay because the paper believed that the man needed more money to support his family. When she moved to the *Indianapolis Star*, Kreuscher found that she had far less freedom for enterprise than she had had at the *Journal*. Today she is an attorney in Indianapolis.

Women continued to play leading roles in family newspaper businesses such as the chain of weeklies run by Loral and Elna Johnson of Imperial that employs three of their four children.

The Johnsons joined the *Imperial Republican* in 1954 and purchased it in 1968. Later they bought the *Holyoke (CO) Enterprise*, the *Wauneta Breeze*, and the *Grant Tribune-Sentinel*. Although Elna served as society editor for the Imperial paper and covered other stories, she focused on managing the chain. She became president of the Nebraska Press Association in 1993, a position her husband had previously held, and also received the national Emma C. McKinney Award for her contributions to weekly journalism. Ironically neither she nor Bev Pollock, Nebraska's other McKinney Award winner, is in the NPA Hall of Fame, although both of their husbands are. By the mid-1970s a few younger family teams were entering weekly journalism, such as Maxine and Francis Moul, who started Maverick Media, a chain of weeklies and shoppers in southeast Nebraska that was headquartered in Syracuse. Their company drew considerable attention because both Mouls were political activists who were McGovern delegates at the 1972 Democratic Convention. Maxine Moul later served as lieutenant governor under Governor Ben Nelson and has held a series of important state, private, and federal economic development positions.

Newspaper and broadcasting sports departments remained male bastions long after news departments opened to women — and Husker football was the biggest bastion of all. Lynne Grasz, later a CBS Broadcasting Group official in New York, said that in 1964 she was the first woman to report from the Memorial Stadium press box for KNUS, the student radio station. She also wrote a story about it for the NU Alumni Association that was never published. She recalled that her classmate Peggy Speece was denied her ambition to become a sports photographer because the Big Eight banned women in slacks and jeans from the sidelines at football games; officials also would not allow a woman to wear a dress because they felt it was "inappropriate for bending on the sidelines."

NATIONALLY PROMINENT BOOMER JOURNALISTS:
LYNNE GRASZ AND TRUDY LIEBERMAN

As Nebraska women journalists had for a century, some left the state for top national jobs. These included Grasz, a former director of communications for the CBS Broadcast Group who runs her own public relations firm in New York, and Trudy Lieberman, a pioneer consumer reporter and longtime contributing editor for the *Columbia Journalism Review*. Grasz, a Lincoln native, had always dreamed of reporting for CBS News in New York but got a hint of how hard this would be when she interviewed top national broadcasters for an NU in-depth reporting assignment in 1965. CBS News president Richard Salant told her he would "*never* hire a woman to do on-air news" because women lacked an air of authority and would not be believed during a national crisis. He also rejected hiring women because he said they had irritating, high-pitched voices that are not strong and commanding and that they get irritable once a month. Pauline Frederick, who covered the United Nations for NBC News, warned Grasz that she would have to sacrifice marriage and motherhood, the same message J-School director William Hall frequently gave women. "He [Hall] wanted us all to be serious professionals and not waste our education on a marriage. As a woman you could *not* have a career and a marriage and/or family. You had to be able to go for the story, with no strings."

Grasz was undeterred partially because her mother had always told her that she had the "ability to be anything [she] wanted to be," so she systematically advanced toward her goal of a New York media career beginning with interning for United Press International in Omaha during college. After graduation in 1966 she joined UPI in Detroit, where she earned a national byline for covering a Beatles concert as a "girl in the crowd." She soon returned to Lincoln as promotion director for KOLN/KGIN-TV, and in 1977, she was elected president of the Broadcasters Promotion Association, the first woman to head a national broadcast trade association. This led to a position as director of information services for KMOX-TV in Saint Louis, a CBS-owned and operated station. In 1981 Grasz finally realized her dream when she became director of communication for the CBS Broadcast Group in New York City. There she discovered that the glass ceiling within CBS limited further advancement, so she took the advice of CBS Broadcast Group president Gene Jankowski, who told her that "sometimes the way up a ladder is to get on the rung of another ladder." She left CBS to manage three different broadcast industry trade associations before deciding to "make money for [herself] instead of others."

In 1991 she founded Grasz Communications, an international PR firm, many of whose clients have links to Nebraska such as Lincoln's International Quilt Study Center and Museum. They seek Grasz's expertise because she has national media connections, understands Nebraska, and returns to Lincoln frequently to visit her mother. Calling Nebraskans "the original networkers," Grasz said, "We help our neighbors. Our word is our bond. We've got a strong pioneer work ethic and a sense that we want to do our best because we don't want to disappoint people who trust us. Nebraskans are very supportive of each other. I can't imagine coming from any other state." Throughout her career Grasz has received numerous top national broadcasting and service awards, including the Distinguished Alumni award from the NU Alumni Association. It cited her work with the association's Cather Circle (comprised of outstanding women alums), which she has chaired, and her work in mentoring young women from Nebraska who aspire to media careers in New York. In 2011 she became a charter member of the Nebraska Press Women's Hall of Fame.

Grasz is not alone in believing that her Nebraska values have helped advance her career. Trudy Lieberman, one of the nation's first consumer reporters and a journalistic authority on health care, feels that she has had an advantage over some of her colleagues with Ivy League backgrounds because her childhood in Scottsbluff taught her how to relate to people of all types. This has been a significant asset in her forty years of interviewing "the little guy" about the problems she has investigated. Lieberman, the daughter of a Polish-immigrant junk peddler, decided to become a newspaper reporter during junior high school because she believed it would allow her to make a difference as her father urged her to do. "When I was a kid, he would always say, 'You need to be seen and be heard,' and I grew up believing I could have a significant impact on the world." After hearing John Kennedy's inaugural address, she was even more determined to "make the world a better place." She majored in home economics and journalism at NU, excellent preparation for becoming the first consumer reporter at the *Detroit Free Press*. Creating a consumer beat was part of that paper's groundbreaking effort to revolutionize its women's news section and provide readers with substantive information on issues affecting women and families.

One of Lieberman's first assignments was to determine if anger over mistreatment by merchants and banks had fueled Detroit's rioting during the late 1960s. After interviewing numerous residents of low-income neighborhoods about their difficulties, she learned that this was true. "It gave me a great feeling to report on the problems of the little guy." In 1977 she moved to New York to become an investigative reporter for *Consumer Reports*, specializing in economics. Lieberman now writes about healthcare issues for the *Columbia Journalism Review* in addition to teaching media courses at several colleges, but she still enjoys talking to ordinary people on the street to get their perspective on health care, social security, and other issues. She especially enjoys sampling grassroots opinion outside New York City to gain a broader perspective on issues.

Lieberman traces the roots of her success to the values of honesty, respect for people regardless of their status, and hard work that she absorbed in Scottsbluff, where, she said, "you learn to do what's right and that has made me a successful journalist because you can figure out what's wrong pretty quickly. You can see injustice." The diversity of people she knew in Scottsbluff has also contributed to her success because unlike many of her Ivy League–educated colleagues from privileged backgrounds, she grew up knowing people who struggled to buy food. As a result she can relate to all types of people, something the "Ivy League people can't do." Throughout her career she has received twenty-six national and regional reporting awards and has written five books, including *Slanting the Story*, an assessment of the impact of conservative think tanks and lobbying organizations on news reporting.

WOMEN'S NEWS CHANGES LITTLE

Because things changed so radically during the course of this decade, it seemed logical to sample a week of women's news from the *World-Herald* in 1961 and a comparable week from the pivotal year of 1968, with its major events such as the Tet Offensive and the assassinations of Martin Luther King Jr. and Robert Kennedy. The first week in May seemed a good choice because that's when the crucial Nebraska primary was held in 1968. An examination of the microfilm showed major changes in the news sections over the seven intervening years but little change in women's news, where weddings, social tidbits, food, and fashion continued to fill the skimpy space allotted to the section except for Sundays and food days.

The news columns provide a better glimpse of the lives of women even if they appear as bit players in 1961 papers dominated by war, politics, and economics. Men may have dominated the news but not the population. The 1960 census shows that there were more females than males in Nebraska and thirty-eight other states. The article "Respectable Spinsterhood Needed to Balance Census" reflected on the problems this caused. Fortunately "marriageable girls didn't need to worry about finding husbands" because of the equal numbers of young boys and girls. The "problem" reflected women's longer life spans; older women could expect a "manless existence." The news sections also featured "queens" of several varieties who got their due, ranging from the "12 Pretty Finalists" for Miss Omaha to the "Spelling Queen" who celebrated her victory in the Midwest Spelling Bee by demanding a hamburger. The winner of the National Science Fair International was saluted as "an energetic, attractive belle from Tennessee" who also happened to be good at science. A few stories spotlighted the activities of professional women such as the fund drive that Nebraska nurses launched to improve nursing services. In line with the state's ongoing concern about its brain drain (including women), the state Department of Education found that Nebraska was losing its college-educated elementary teachers to other states more than twice as fast as the average of other states.

By 1968 one obvious change in the news section is the appearance of two female bylines. Mary McGrath wrote a story about the Nixon family's campaign stop in Omaha, while Susan Harr wrote a Teen Page story headlined "Students Get a Taste of Political Campaign." Women's news carried only one story that even mentioned politics: "Wed Club to Have Political Party." Not all news section coverage of women could be considered substantive, as the adjacent stories on the coronation of NU's May Queen and *Playboy* magazine's 1967 Playmate of the Year illustrate. On a front page filled with pre-primary news, a headline labeled "For the Women" also jumped out: "Shoppers Should Read to Enter This Market." The lead reads: "Women have proved they know how to make money. Many a husband will tell you they know how to spend it. But do women know how to invest money?" Two women's news stories reflect the section's traditional orientation. The article headlined "Straight A Student Stitches Seams Straight" told readers, "Add this story to the credit side of the ledger on the record of the younger generation in this year of the protest, the sit-in and the draft card burner." It seems that a straight-A Iowa State University senior had made her wedding dress, going-away costume, and dresses for two of her attendants and her flower girl. Another story reassured "ample females" that "Plump Girls Have Success in Marriage, Report Says," but offered numerous suggestions for either slimming down or appearing trimmer.

This random sampling of coverage reminds us that most Nebraskans, including young people, lived traditional lives throughout the 1960s regardless of what was happening politically. In 1968 the changes that the women's movement would bring remained a few years in the future, although there were hints of things to come such as McGrath's breaking into city news at the *World-Herald*. However, no fortune-teller could have predicted how much the generation beginning to graduate from college in the late 1960s would change life for women in all fields, including journalism.

9 | Women Journalists of Color

Until modern times Omaha's African Americans suffered from segregation in jobs and housing nearly as pervasive as that of the South. Blacks came to Omaha with the earliest settlers and have "deeper roots than those of many of the immigrant groups." They found service jobs with the railroads and hotels but were denied access to many fields and for decades were confined to segregated neighborhoods in North and South Omaha. To this day a large economic gap remains between blacks and whites in Omaha.

Omaha's most notorious outbreak of race hatred was the courthouse riot of 1919, when a mob stormed the county jail and lynched William Brown, an African American prisoner accused of rape. Mayor Edward Smith, who tried to end the violence and protect Brown, was rescued from being lynched himself at the last instant. The growth of Omaha's African American population to over ten thousand during World War I fueled the riot because some of the newcomers took jobs in the packinghouses formerly held by whites who had gone to war. The return of veterans and the competition for jobs increased hostility toward blacks. Black economic fortunes declined even further during the 1930s, when the Depression dried up "opportunities for blacks . . . in direct relationship to rising white unemployment." By 1940 African Americans made up about 5 percent of Omaha's population, mostly concentrated in a confined area of North Omaha with another black neighborhood near the South Omaha packinghouses.

After World War II three activists collaborated in launching Omaha's civil rights battle: Mildred Brown, publisher of the

Omaha Star; Whitney Young, a future national head of the Urban League; and the Reverend John Markoe, sj, a Creighton University Jesuit priest. Brown battled race discrimination for fifty years through her paper, which served the African American community. Young, who became head of Nebraska's Urban League in 1950, enlisted several white business leaders in the fight against discrimination in jobs, housing, public facilities, and public education. Markoe founded the interracial DePorres Club, which marched and protested against segregation. But progress was slow. Numerous local businesses would not hire African Americans except in menial positions, many restaurants would not serve people of color, and schools were mostly segregated along with churches and social organizations. The *Omaha World-Herald* did not carry African American social news, although the sports pages featured the achievements of talented future Hall of Fame athletes like Saint Louis Cardinals pitcher Bob Gibson and Chicago Bears running back Gale Sayers, both products of the North Omaha YMCA sports programs run by Gibson's brother.

During the 1960s rioting sparked by continuing discrimination in jobs and housing and complaints about the police erupted several times, notably in 1966 and 1968. Blacks initiated economic development programs with the backing of government, church, and business leaders, the Ford Foundation underwrote a black group's purchase of radio station KOWH, and a black-owned bank opened. The mainstream media hired a few minority journalists and began to cover the grievances and accomplishments of African Americans in addition to crime and sports. Black neighborhoods gained representation on the city council with the change from at-large to district elections pushed by state senator Ernie Chambers. But despite these achievements and the peaceful desegregation of the Omaha Public Schools in the 1970s, race has remained a major local issue. In 2009 Omaha had the third-highest black poverty rate among the nation's top one hundred cities despite its overall wealth and low unemployment rate. It also had one of the nation's highest black homicide rates.

There were few such racial tensions in the rest of Nebraska during this era because Lincoln had only a small African American community and there were hardly any people of color in the rural communities, although occasional families found their way to small towns like Nebraska City. Many rural Nebraskans never saw a black person unless they visited Omaha, so this chapter focuses on that city.

For generations Omaha African Americans seeking a black viewpoint on local racial problems as well as news about their community such as engagements, weddings, club meetings, and church gatherings turned to Mildred Brown's *Omaha Star*, where they found news and views that mainstream media ignored. Brown, who eventually won national recognition for her groundbreaking achievements, offered a combination of activism and North Omaha community coverage. In 1965 President Lyndon Johnson hailed Brown as "the only black woman who was the owner-founder of a black newspaper still in existence" after meeting her at a national publishers meeting. He appointed her as a "goodwill ambassador" to East Germany to study human rights violations connected with the Berlin Wall.

Brown, who died in 1989, inspired young African Americans to consider media careers, including Cathy Hughes and Cheryl Parks Butler, both groundbreakers in their own right. Hughes founded Radio One, the nation's largest African American broadcasting company and is often called the most powerful woman in broadcasting. Butler became the first African American woman on the news staff of a major Nebraska newspaper when she joined the *Lincoln Evening Journal* in 1967. She later spent years as an editor with the *Washington Post*. Eve Goodwin Christian was hired as the first *World-Herald* minority woman city news reporter in the early 1970s.

Hughes, whose father's accounting business was located at the

Star, said Brown had enormous impact on her community. She was not only a successful business owner and a powerful voice for North Omaha but also a "flamboyant presence." Her bright-colored, perfectly coordinated coats, dresses, shoes, purses, and turban-shaped hats complemented by the carnation corsage she always wore stood out in any gathering. Although Brown is Nebraska's most notable African American publisher, she was far from the first.

Oddly, Nebraska's first African American paper was published in Hastings in central Nebraska in the 1870s, an area almost devoid of blacks today. However, little is known about it. Lincoln, which has long had a small African American community, also had an African American paper. Omaha has had ten African American publications, including the *Black Woman's Aurora Magazine*, published for a short time by Lucille Skaggs Edwards, wife of an Omaha dentist, in the early 1900s. The *Star* is the only survivor. All the papers prior to the *Star* concentrated on national political news about African Americans, while Brown focused on the lives and problems of Omaha's black community. "This is where Brown made it," said historian Amy Forss, who wrote her doctoral dissertation on the publisher. "She was all about the community. Because she was a business woman, she knew what sold and she knew people wanted to see their names in the paper." Throughout her life she upheld the newspaper's motto: "Dedicated to the service of the people that no good cause shall lack a champion, and that evil shall not thrive unopposed."

Brown, a native of Bessemer, Alabama, came to Omaha from Sioux City, Iowa, in 1937 with her then-husband Shirl Edward Gilbert. The couple had founded the *Silent Messenger* in Sioux City in 1935 after their pastor told Mildred that the Lord wanted her to start a newspaper. The pastor had noticed her talent for sales and fundraising. When the Gilberts moved to Omaha, Mildred was advertising manager of the *Omaha Guide* newspaper before the couple founded the weekly *Omaha Star* in 1938. Since the 1940s the paper has been located in a former mortuary in the heart of North Omaha's business district that is on the National Register of Historic Places. Although Mildred's skill at selling advertising made the paper successful, her marriage ended in 1943. She resumed her maiden name, took over the paper, and lived in its building for the rest of her life, while Gilbert moved to Kansas City. Despite the divorce the two remained on warm terms.

Brown established her identity as a publisher through an open letter to the community saying, "The *Omaha Star* is your newspaper and brings you each week accurate news concerning the social, civic, religious and economical activities of our group both local and national." She demanded equal employment opportunities even though many whites and some blacks labeled her a troublemaker. The FBI kept an eye on her and the *Star*, as it did on many black publishers. "They thought she had Communist ties," said Forss. During World War II the paper editorialized against segregation of the armed forces and urged readers to apply for jobs at the massive Glenn Martin bomber plant in Bellevue. Employers who discriminated felt Brown's sting. Her front page carried the names of businesses that discriminated, and she participated in the national "Don't Buy Where You Can't Work" campaign. She urged readers to picket local stores that did not hire blacks, and she participated in sit-ins and protest marches. Ironically Brown needed to sell ads to some of the same businesses that she was targeting for their employment practices, and she lost some revenue as a result, Forss noted. Brown also collaborated with Young and Markoe in their efforts to desegregate Omaha. When Creighton told the DePorres Club to meet off campus, she provided meeting space.

During the civil rights struggles of the 1960s, banner headlines in the *Star* told readers about protest meetings, marches, demands to city officials, and their responses. More than ever the *Star* became North Omaha's voice for change. Reporters included local civil rights leaders such as Charles B. Washington, who actually wrote many of the front-page editorials. Historians can tell which editorials Brown personally wrote because she signed her name to them. Two editorials following outbreaks of violence give modern readers a flavor of the newspaper's advocacy journalism.

After North Omaha's Fourth of July riots in 1966, the *Omaha Star* responded with a front-page editorial criticizing rioting but above all demanding action to address protesters' grievances.

> We cannot commend the methods they used to draw attention to the fact that they were frustrated and despaired because they could not feel or see any appreciable betterment of their lot. Likewise we cannot commend those who have failed over the past three years to listen to the traditional methods of calling attention to the fact that in Omaha there is discrimination in housing, education, employment and health and welfare services. But we must hasten to remind that the Boston Tea Party participants, Carrie Nation, Samuel Gompers using similar methods, are not considered now as having been hoodlums. We think that less attention should be paid to the methods they used in calling attention to their plight and more to finding some solutions to the causes which brought their actions about.

The *Star* took a similar stance in a March 7, 1968, front-page editorial about the upheavals that followed a presidential campaign appearance by segregationist governor George Wallace of Alabama. An off-duty police officer killed a black teen in the aftermath of the incident, and unlike the mayor Brown did not think the police had handled the situation "superbly." The editorial's rhetorical questions leave no doubt about the *Star*'s stance:

> Did the police handle the protest at the American Party's confab at Civic Auditorium as "superbly" as claimed by Mayor

A. V. Sorensen? The report [of the National Advisory Commission on Civil Disorder] quotes an off-the-record comment of a member of the City's Legal Department, who was present at the Convention, that "the police could have handled it a lot differently." The report . . . contains a charge by an official of the Nebraska-for-McCarthy group that Wallace and his aides were the ones who should have been arrested and charged with disrupting a public meeting, a charge which has been filed in Municipal Court against two Catholic priests.

Brown's stature in the black community was demonstrated when rioters who burned and vandalized other North Omaha businesses in 1966 spared the *Star*. Some of this reflected the fact that Brown never forgot that she was running the equivalent of a small-town weekly where people liked to see their names in print. No matter what the political news, the *Star* always featured weddings and engagements, announcements of church services, club news, fashion advice, obituaries, and even black-themed comics. Every issue also focused on the accomplishments of local African Americans, sometimes juxtaposed on the same page with news of racial violence. The July 22, 1966, issue offers such an example. A page 1 obituary eulogized Florentine Pinkerton, a piano teacher who had graduated from the New England Conservatory of Music and studied in France. Nearby was a story about Mayor Sorensen's call for more action to stop the riots. Brown's push for readers and advertisers also was apparent. To attract readers in Lincoln, she carried columns of black social news from that city. Even less subtle were her front-page editorial calls for businesses to reach their black customers by advertising in the *Omaha Star*.

Eventually some 150 groups honored Brown, including the NAACP, which presented her with its "Unsung Heroine" service award in 1981. As she got older, she refused to retire, saying, "I'll be at the *Omaha Star* until God takes me." In the years since her sudden death in 1989, recognition has continued. The Nebraska Press Association elected her to its Hall of Fame in 2007, as did the Nebraska Press Women in 2012. In 2008 the City of Omaha opened the Mildred Brown Strolling Park near the *Omaha Star* office. There is also a Mildred Brown Street, and the Mildred Brown Scholarship assists Creighton University journalism students of color. Brown's impact continues to be felt in the lives she touched such as Hughes's.

"I witnessed firsthand the power of the press," said Hughes, who began her career by selling ads for the *Star* when she was only twelve. "She was an activist and an amazing person. She had a militant stance. The *Star* was a proactive militant publication, and she was unique on top of it all." Hughes said she saw the media as a field she wanted to be part of and Brown as a model of activism that has inspired her throughout her own radio career. Brown also had an impact on Butler, whose mother, Mary Parks, worked in the *Omaha Star's* office. Parks's love of newspapers was a factor in Butler's decision to study journalism, although mainstream Nebraska media were just beginning to hire their first minority news staffers (male) when she was a student at Central High School.

FROM THE *CENTRAL HIGH SCHOOL REGISTER* TO THE *WASHINGTON POST*

As a senior working on the *Central High School Register*, Butler won a state journalism award, then became the only African American at the University of Nebraska "J-School" when she majored in journalism. She has fond memories of faculty members such as R. Neale Copple, director of the school, and James Morrison, who taught typography. Like most J-School students, she interned during the summer, but her summer stint at the *Beatrice Sun* introduced her to a community that had only one black family. She lived with a white woman who "made [her] feel at home" and covered events that were strange to her, such as a 4-H livestock show. This event taught the city girl to focus photos on the winning cow, not its proud owner. "It [Beatrice] was much quieter than Omaha and a way to learn that everyone is not the same. It was a good experience for me to be away from home."

When Butler graduated from the university, she did not apply for a job at the *Omaha World-Herald* because "it wasn't hospitable to blacks. The *World-Herald* wrote crime stories but ignored the lives of African Americans." Instead she took a job on the *Lincoln Evening Journal* copy desk during her final semester of college, then became wire editor in 1967. She was apparently the first African American woman journalist on a mainstream Nebraska newspaper. Her job involved selecting national news stories from wire services, writing headlines, and laying out pages; it was especially demanding in 1968, when Martin Luther King and Robert Kennedy were assassinated and demonstrators clashed with police at the Democratic National Convention. "There was so much work to do. The *Journal* had so many wire services, not just the AP and UPI but the *Chicago Daily News* and the *New York Times*." Butler's four years at the *Journal* under the supervision of managing editor Gilbert Savery taught her to handle a complex editing job, and she remains grateful to Savery, "a wonderful boss and a good mentor" who "knew his stuff and gave [her] confidence."

In 1972 Butler became a copy editor at the *Saint Paul Dispatch*, then joined the *Washington Post* in 1981 as a makeup editor. She participated in the transition to electronic layouts and was involved in the coverage of numerous major stories. After becoming director of recruiting in 2000, she traveled widely interviewing potential employees and interns, seeking to increase the newsroom's diversity. She retired in 2004 and has remained in the Washington area, although she returns to Omaha to visit her family. Butler credits Central High's outstanding advanced placement English and math classes for laying the groundwork for her success. "I learned so much there. I felt sorry coming to Washington about how bad public education is." In heavily African American Washington, she was viewed as exotic because of her Nebraska roots. Easterners were surprised to discover that Nebraska even had African Americans and tended to confuse Omaha with Oklahoma City. "It makes you humble." However, Butler said her Nebraska roots have given her a useful perspective for surviving the "rat race" of the capital. "The whole world does not depend on what Washington does. People in the Midwest know how to treat people. The worldview is different. People are more polite and more friendly. That's the way things get done."

THE *OMAHA WORLD-HERALD* REACHES OUT

Although Butler had followed a traditional path into journalism, she was a rarity in Nebraska. Few African American area students studied journalism because discrimination limited their job opportunities, but that situation was changing because the civil rights movement taught major news organizations that it was important to diversify their news staffs. In order to recruit minority journalists, they turned to special programs such as one at Columbia University in which Eve Goodwin Christian participated en route to becoming the *Omaha World-Herald's* first African American woman reporter. By the time Christian joined the paper in 1970, the *World-Herald* had hired several African American men reporters who stayed for only a few years and photographer Rudy Smith, who spent his entire distinguished career at the paper.

In the late 1960s Christian, a member of a prominent black Omaha family who had received her degree in sociology at Creighton University, was working at a child-care facility while studying for a master's degree in social work when she was offered the chance to become a journalist. The Ford Foundation selected 30 scholarship recipients from 350 applicants nationally to do graduate work in journalism at Columbia in a program run by former CBS News president Fred Friendly as part of an effort to combat racial violence nationally. Christian had filled out the lengthy application almost on impulse. Step 2 was a personal interview and a writing tryout with a reporter from the *San Francisco Examiner* who came to Omaha. "We went into a room at the *World-Herald* with a typewriter and they asked me to write something. I did. He liked it. They invited me to participate." She was sponsored by the *World-Herald*, which guaranteed her a job, another criterion for acceptance. Christian's fellow participants in the three-month program included future TV star Geraldo Rivera, who then went by "Gerry." Noted journalists from various papers taught the classes, and assignments were often in nearby Harlem, an adventure for a young woman from Omaha. "At the end we had a big celebration. [Civil rights leader] Julian Bond spoke."

In September 1970 Christian became a *World-Herald* reporter. A warm and vivacious person, she was comfortable being the only African American woman at the paper because she had attended mostly white Catholic schools and was "always in settings where [she] was the only one [person of color]. African American people are often thrust into those roles. It's a way of life. You almost expect it." She quickly made friends with "the whole young group" at the paper, especially the women. "I was on general assignment and education I would go out to the schools." However, she was uncomfortable with reporting as an occupation because she did not want to write about things that she did not see as stories just because her bosses did. She also was ill at ease with the brevity of most news stories because she was more concerned about good writing. "This is why I knew that news reporting was not for me long term. Writing was my strength." She resigned after two years to move to Washington DC to marry her husband, lawyer Clyde Christian. They returned to Omaha to raise their family after their twins were born, and Christian has held a variety of jobs in addition to writing short stories. When I interviewed her in 2010, she was working on a novel.

FROM OMAHA TO RADIO ONE

About the same time that Butler and Christian were growing up in Omaha, one of the nation's most powerful women in broadcasting, Cathy Hughes, decided that she would become a national radio star, and she prepared for it by practicing "broadcasting" at her home in North Omaha's Logan Fontenelle public housing project. "I was going to be the first black with a nationally syndicated radio show. I would lock the bathroom door and use my toothbrush as a microphone." Her family of six did not appreciate having the unit's sole bathroom tied up this way in the morning, but nothing could deter the future founder of the nation's largest African American broadcast company. Years later she learned that Academy Award winner Hattie McDaniel had already had a national radio show, but Hughes would compile her own impressive list of firsts.

Although Hughes's heart was set on radio rather than print like her role model Brown, she followed Brown's activist model from the start. She joined the NAACP Youth Council while attending Duchesne Academy, a Catholic girls' high school. She helped raise her classmates' consciousness, and some of them were arrested with her when the NAACP attempted to integrate the segregated Peony Park swimming area in a white neighborhood. Hughes had been swimming there with her Duchesne classmates without problems, but that changed when the NAACP youth group joined them to confront the issue and arrests followed. At sixteen her life changed when she became pregnant with her son, Alfred Liggins III, but she still graduated from high school in 1964.

Hughes had a sporadic post–high school education, but as a student in the University of Nebraska at Omaha's black studies program, she became acquainted with Tony Brown, dean of Howard University's School of Communications in Washington DC and host of PBS's *Black Journal*. Brown had formed strong ties with Omaha's black community and made a number of appear-

ances at UNO with the encouragement of one of his fans, Susan
Buffett, wife of financier Warren Buffett. Brown was impressed
with Hughes's volunteer work at KOWH, Omaha's black radio station, where she learned the basics of radio operations, and in
1972 he hired her to lecture at Howard. In addition to lecturing
Hughes became general sales manager of Howard's radio station
and later was promoted to general manager and vice president.
She also created "Quiet Storm," the most listened to nighttime
radio format, which featured a variation on rhythm and blues.
But Hughes wanted independence. She had been amazed to discover that Washington DC had no black-owned radio station and
set out to change that.

In 1979 she and her husband Dewey Hughes purchased a troubled radio station, WOL-AM, moved it from Georgetown to a
black neighborhood, and converted it to a talk-radio station.
However, trying to turn the station around was such a financial
struggle that it ended the marriage, and Dewey moved to California, while Cathy tried to keep the station afloat. She and her
son lost their home and car and moved to a makeshift apartment
in the radio station. She even sold a rare heirloom white-gold
pocket watch made by slaves for fifty thousand dollars to stave
off her creditors. Her determination paid off when the station
showed a profit seven years later. Like Brown, Hughes advocated
for controversial black causes. For example, she accused the
Washington Post of biased reporting in the case of a rap artist accused of murder, and eventually the *Post*'s publisher and editor
appeared on her show to apologize. Even as she engaged in political controversy, Hughes expanded her business by moving
into FM radio, buying troubled stations around the country, and
turning them around. Her son joined her in the business, and
today he is CEO of Radio One and she is chairperson. In 2010
Radio One owned more than fifty stations and partnered with
Comcast Corporation on a subsidiary, TV One, that competes
with BET in African American cable programming. Hughes is

the first African American woman to head a publicly traded company and has been called the nation's most powerful woman in radio. Numerous groups have honored her and Liggins. In 2005 she became the Time Warner Endowed Chair of Howard University's Department of Radio, Television, and Film.

Looking back on her career and the impact of growing up in Omaha's African American community, Hughes cited its relatively small size and the influence of strong leaders like Brown, Washington, Chambers, and star musicians like Preston Love. Omaha had "so few black people that [they] all knew each other. There was a collective push forward." Hughes said that she knows that lifelong friends are following her career and expect excellence from her, and commented, "To this day I am inspired to do great things."

A REFLECTION ON WOMEN OF COLOR AND MEDIA

Unlike most chapters in this one it isn't necessary to present examples from local mainstream newspaper microfilm to depict how the women spotlighted lived. Although this chapter incorporates examples of Brown's journalism, I saw no point in searching *World-Herald* microfilm to obtain portrayals of African American women prior to the late 1960s because all the reams of microfilm studied for other chapters contained no significant coverage of African American women in women's news. African Americans interviewed for this book still recall their exclusion from the social columns for accounts of events, club meetings, engagements, and weddings.

By the time I joined the *Omaha World-Herald* in 1969 as religion reporter, city news welcomed stories about African Americans, and my church page was filled with announcements of African American church events. Churches were major forces in the efforts to improve economic conditions in North Omaha, so I wrote numerous features about developments and the people behind them in addition to the items about routine church events, precisely the kind of mundane community news that had previously been excluded. I also began reading the *Omaha Star* and met Mildred Brown several times. I recall her as a formidable figure who changed the tone of any room she entered. My news sources taught me about the tense relationship between the *World-Herald* and the African American community. It helped explain their wariness that receded after several fair and accurate stories. About this time, the Women's News Department also opened the social announcements to African American news but understandably never announced the change because this would have required acknowledging past exclusion. It took time but gradually blacks began to submit more community news items and the social columns began routinely printing them.

As a final personal note, I worked with both Butler and Christian at the *Lincoln Evening Journal* and *Omaha World-Herald*, respectively. As an intern on the *Journal* copy desk in the summer of 1968, it was almost intimidating to watch Butler calmly working the wires during the horrible week of the RFK assassination. Christian became a friend the day that she marched into the *World-Herald* and was assigned the desk next to mine. Evie and I remained friends after she left the paper and have reconnected sporadically. Her brother Alvin Goodwin Jr., a key figure in North Omaha economic development work and a good news source, opened the door for my interview with Cathy Hughes.

In retrospect it is shocking to realize that Cheryl and Evie became the first women of color in Nebraska's mainstream media less than fifty years ago. This fact alone attests to how recently women of color faced dual barriers in Nebraska journalism. Black women did not begin appearing on local TV news until even later, outside the time frame of this book. Trina Creighton, now a faculty member at the University of Nebraska–Lincoln College of Journalism, may have been the first when she joined KMTV in the late 1970s.

10 | Integrating Omaha Media

By 1970 Omaha was a city on the verge of major changes. It remained Nebraska's financial engine housing the corporate headquarters for such major companies as Union Pacific Railroad, Mutual of Omaha, Northwestern Bell Telephone, and Northern Natural Gas and was noted for its wealth thanks partially to legendary investor Warren Buffett. Peter Kiewit, head of Kiewit Construction Company, dominated the business community and provided overall civic leadership as well. He had purchased the *Omaha World-Herald* to prevent a chain from buying it because he believed that chain newspapers were bad for their communities, and he didn't want that to happen in Omaha.

Omaha had been shaken by the racial disturbances of the 1960s, and leaders worried about the city's deteriorating downtown as retailers vacated grand old buildings to move to the shopping centers in the suburbs. In South Omaha the stockyards declined as meatpackers moved to rural areas closer to livestock producers. To combat the deterioration Mayor Eugene Leahy proposed an ambitious Riverfront Development program that slowly transformed the downtown area over the next forty years through a combination of public improvements and private investments. On a smaller scale the Mercer family began converting the old fruit and vegetable city market warehouses adjacent to downtown into restaurants, specialty shops, and loft apartments, saving this picturesque area from destruction. Gradually the Old Market morphed from a haven for hippies into an upscale tourist attraction convenient to the hotels, concert hall, parks, and convention center that were among the centerpieces of Riverfront Development.

Ironically Omaha's domination by business and its well-paid corporate jobs probably impeded the professional integration of women because breakthroughs were usually easier with employers who paid less. This was true in media as in other fields. Several decades later, men still dominated top management positions citywide, although women had become well integrated at upper-middle management and lower levels. Omaha baby boom women nearing retirement, however, could take pride in the employment barriers they had broken and the improvements in social services for women and girls. The glass ceiling remained, but the cracks kept growing.

Most Friday evenings in the late 1960s, *Omaha World-Herald* education reporter Fred Thomas faced writing stacks of one- and two-paragraph "shorts" for the Sunday paper before he could take off for the weekend. His friend Mary McGrath, who covered clubs and wrote features in the women's news section, started helping him when she was caught up with her own work. It was a small gesture but one that led to the opening of city news to women at Nebraska's most important newspaper. When Thomas became city editor in 1967, he transferred McGrath to "cityside," making her the first full-time woman in city news since the end of World War II. Call it integration via "short" instead of "suit." Within a few more years Omaha TV stations also began hiring women reporters such as Rose Ann Shannon, Carol Schrader, and Ann Pedersen.

Such virtually invisible expansion of opportunities typifies the way that women integrated major newspapers throughout the Midwest rather than through the East Coast's headline-making lawsuits, said Scott Bosley, executive director of the American Society of Newspaper Editors. EEO laws had less impact on creating new opportunities for women journalists on newspapers than did economics and changing expectations. Even major regional newspapers faced talent shortages due partially to the Vietnam War draft. Women journalism graduates who "felt they could do anything anyone else could" jumped at the opportunities because "they were committed to journalism and its place in society and they expected to succeed." Many were determined to prove themselves in hard news now that they had the chance.

Once hired, women in midsized markets like Omaha throughout the country who encountered sex discrimination seldom sued their employers as women did at the *New York Times* because this meant career suicide if a woman had no plans to move, said Bosley. There were only a handful of media employers in cities the size of Omaha (metro area at the time: about 750,000), and they could informally punish malcontents of either sex by making daily life miserable. Shannon, now news director of KETV, took a dim view of confrontations; she stated, "I always found I was working for reasonable people. Confrontation was not productive. We could resolve differences through channels." Rather than complain about sexism that men did not perceive, women in all forms of media tended to raise specific points, then retreat into humor if the reaction was too negative. Less than ten years after McGrath's transfer to city news, a cohort of young women who supported each other informally through organizations like the Omaha Press Club had integrated all major Omaha media employers. During these years of change, McGrath was a steadying influence on the growing number of young women at the *World-Herald* and a role model for those in TV.

MARY MCGRATH: GROUNDBREAKER AND MENTOR

Growing up in Gretna near Omaha, McGrath often visited the *Gretna Breeze* with a playmate whose family owned the paper. "I was fascinated by what was going on. It was my earliest newspaper influence." At home she and her brother, Tony, spread the *World-Herald* out on the carpet and read it page by page. McGrath majored in journalism at Creighton University and edited the student newspaper, the *Creightonian*. She became a reporter at the *Council Bluffs Nonpareil* after graduating in 1956, commuting from her Omaha home by bus because she did not own a car. Helping cover major stories such as a nursing-home fire was satisfying, and her first love always was news. However, catching a bus home late at night was so difficult that she took a women's news job at the *World-Herald* in 1957. At least she got her foot in the door. After transferring to city news, McGrath covered the Henry Doorly Zoo, the library, and school district 66 before focusing increasingly on medicine and health, her beat for more than twenty years. Her best-known articles included an in-depth portrait of a doctor coping with cancer and an investigation of an abortion at the University of Nebraska Medical Center in which the baby was born alive. She shared the state's top AP award for the latter story with noted investigative reporter Robert Dorr.

McGrath also mentored younger women reporters and female interns. Every summer she invited the interns to dinner to explain the newsroom environment, especially as they grew more vocally feminist during the early 1970s. "I wanted them to understand that they were coming into a professional environment that was different than a college campus. It was important for them to understand that they didn't have to give up their personal beliefs but they had to express them so they would be understood if they were to make the most of this opportunity. If you were too straightforward with anyone, including the people you worked with, you could turn them off." The interns could easily mistake typical newsroom banter for sexism, she said. Male reporters who kiddingly called female colleagues "sweetheart" were not necessarily chauvinists. Some were far more helpful to women than men who would never have used a casual endearment. Young women hurt themselves professionally by erupting at routine byplay rather than responding in kind.

McGrath also organized potluck dinners to eliminate the barriers between the women in city news and Women's News. She

wanted the female city reporters to appreciate the professionalism of the Women's News Department staff. "In one sense the
potlucks were a hangover from my Creighton days. I went to
Creighton when there were not many women. We learned to
come together and share a sisterhood. On the paper it was important and good for us to share and encourage and support each
other." McGrath remained one of the *World-Herald*'s most respected reporters until her retirement in 2000. Her honors include the Omaha Press Club Foundation's Career Achievement
Award and Creighton University's top alumni award. In 2012 she
was elected to the Nebraska Press Women's Hall of Fame.

INTEGRATING OMAHA TV NEWS

While a veteran reporter opened the door for women at the
World-Herald, interns did this at the city's three TV stations, KMTV,
KETV, and WOW-TV (which became WOWT in 1975), according to
retired photographer David Hamer, who worked for all three
stations. Among those who made a significant impact at the three
stations were Shannon, Schrader, and Pedersen. "Women interns
came in and proved themselves," Hamer said. "They worked a
heck of a lot harder than most of the male interns. This had been
a male environment up to this point, and suddenly we had
women. The older guys were either aloof or protective. Intern-
ships were a route for women to get their foot in the door."

Around 1970 stations began hiring women to do the weather
"as a ploy to boost the ratings. They were picked for their looks
and the stations dressed them," Hamer said. The first was KMTV's
Sheryl Donnermeyer, who went by Donna Meyer and sported
miniskirts and boots on camera. The serious young women journalists breaking in about this time were determined to succeed
on talent, not sex appeal, none more so than Shannon, KMTV's
first full-time woman reporter, who said that colleagues sometimes joked that the station had hired her and an African American photographer as "tokens," a situation that didn't trouble Shan-

non: "We didn't care. We knew we had to prove ourselves." She did this by covering everything — education, housing, medicine, city hall, police, and spot news — with a confidence gained from her teachers at all-girl Marian High School, who had taught her to think big and overcome limitations.

Shannon, a broadcast journalism graduate of UNO who was hired in 1973, said she never faced discrimination but "felt pretty isolated in the early days" until more women were hired. "It would have been tough if I hadn't had the acceptance of the guys. You always knew you were different, but it made you stronger. You didn't make excuses. You just did the job. There were lots of people who wanted these jobs. I think we had something to prove. What's so wonderful about TV is that there are no limitations." She became a press aide to Mayor Mike Boyle in 1985, then moved to assignment editor at KETV in 1986. Since 1993 she has been news director, the station's top job in news. She also has served as chairperson of the ABC Affiliate News Directors' Advisory Board.

Another groundbreaker, former KETV anchor Carol Schrader, also graduated in broadcasting from UNO and interned at KMTV, but her first full-time job was working nights at radio station KLNG. As the station's city hall reporter, she once got into a shouting match with the mayor at his weekly news conference after he falsely accused her of feeding unfounded information to a source, which Schrader denied. KETV, which had taped the incident, then hired her, but she too knew she had to prove herself. "I wasn't a sex symbol. I covered city hall, county board, and spot news. Women were a novelty. We knew we had to work harder and prove ourselves a little bit more than men."

Schrader refused to be deterred from covering any story because she was a woman. During her internship at KMTV, a police officer was killed in a shoot-out that occurred shortly before 10:00 p.m. Schrader asked to go to the crime scene but was told there was "no way" the station would send an intern, let alone a woman, to the shooting. After she got off work at 10:30 p.m., she told her boss she was going to the crime scene anyway, so he sent her to the nearest emergency room where the officer had been taken. She photographed his body being carried in and received an extra payment for her footage. "I insisted on doing something, and I was the only one there." Schrader became KETV's first woman evening coanchor in 1979, a position she held until she left the station in 1996. After working in the county assessor's office, she became a realtor.

WOWT's first woman reporter, Ann Pedersen, a native of Laurel, Nebraska, got her job in 1974 when the star of Romper Room School, who was counted as news staff, resigned, and the station needed a woman to replace her on its EEO report to the FCC. "It was pretty obvious," said Pedersen. "The station was hiring a reporter. The three finalists were three women." Afterward Pedersen succeeded on merit. News director Steve Murphy told his staff, "She's just one of the boys," and "wouldn't have tolerated any kind of discrimination." Pedersen, a UNL broadcasting graduate who had interned at KHOL-TV in central Nebraska and worked for NETV, covered politics, crime, and local government. She recalls flying to North Platte to help cover the Simants murder case in Sutherland, Nebraska, which became the subject of a major U.S. Supreme Court press freedom decision. When she began doing the noon news in 1975, she became the first Omaha woman to anchor a daily newscast. A few years later she became assignment editor, then assistant news director, but left WOWT for WCCO-TV in Minneapolis in 1988. Today she is a public relations writer in Omaha.

EXPANDING THE DEFINITION OF NEWS

Women reporters have made a significant impact through covering stories about women's problems that would never have occurred to their male colleagues, in the process expanding the definition of news. Most stories get into the newspaper or on TV because a reporter hears about something that strikes her or him as newsworthy because it is out of the ordinary, trendy, heart-warming, a problem for many readers/viewers, and so on. When women began breaking into news, male colleagues sometimes dismissed them because they couldn't pick up tips in bars, but by the early 1970s women reporters were getting tips from other women that men could not get about protests against sex discrimination, crusades for better social services, and the unending battle over abortion. As Schrader noted, "Women brought the consequences of facts to the newsroom. I have been very sensitive to how things affect women and children." News operations that drew on the differing perspectives of men and women created "a whole greater than the sum of the parts." Shannon said that even today "some people sneer at the feminization of news," meaning coverage of health, schools, and issues that affect women. However, strong news teams must represent a variety of perspectives. "I'm a huge believer in diversity because everybody sees stories differently and everyone has different news sources. This is so good for a newsroom."

Two veteran male journalists gave examples of the value of adding women's perspectives to news. Dorr cited a series of stories on credit discrimination against women that he would have covered on his business beat had he been aware of the problems. He said he also regrets missing a trend piece on the growth of women-owned businesses. Hamer recalled learning about day-care problems when he teamed up with a reporter-mother for a series of stories, a subject that had not previously been on his radar. He particularly enjoyed photographing a series on a woman's first pregnancy that Pedersen suggested at WOWT. "These would have been great stories no matter who thought of them. They got tremendous attention."

MODERNIZING WOMEN'S NEWS

Although this chapter emphasizes the importance of integrating women into city news, it is important not to slight the efforts of women journalists like *World-Herald* women's news editor Patricia Wolfe to modernize her section, which still employs a significant number of women. Social news has always suffered a stigma. "There's no question that the guys put down Women's News," said Dorr. Ironically the *World-Herald* even assigned city news reporters to cover the city's biggest annual traditional social event, the Ak-Sar-Ben Coronation, although Women's News Department staffers wrote numerous articles leading up to the event and following up on it. But locally and nationally traditional ideas about social news sections were changing with the times. Wolfe envisioned turning women's news into a features section called Living that would appeal equally to women and men since numerous men, including top editors, also read the section. Backed by the excellent staff she was building, Wolfe gradually changed the focus of the section, adding new material to coverage of traditional topics. For example, noted food writer Jane Palmer incorporated information on nutrition into pieces that included recipes. Feature writer Nancy Ellis wrote stories about women achievers that could have appeared anywhere in the paper, and Robyn Carmichael Eden discovered consumer angles in fashion writing that she had never envisioned when she was hired for that assignment in 1970. Women on city news encouraged these efforts at McGrath's potlucks. Even those who arrived at the paper with a disdain for working in women's news came to realize that the staff members who produced it were not responsible for blocking change. The young women journalists that Wolfe had hired greatly respected her efforts to modernize their section. Eden's experience exemplifies Wolfe's transformation of the section even before the transition to Living.

"When I applied to *World-Herald* in 1970, the only opening was for a fashion editor in Women's News," said Eden, a UNO journalism graduate. "I knew nothing about fashion except how my mom told me to dress, which I ignored. I figured I could learn." On her new beat she gained "fascinating insights into how the fashion industry affected people, enjoyed interviewing top designers such as Oscar de la Renta and Bill Blass, and covered consumer safety issues like requirements for flame-retardant pajamas." However, she discovered that "Women's News and City News were separate worlds." "We were thought of as light weights, but we were allowed a certain amount of freedom because no one was looking over our shoulders. We didn't have near the scrutiny of city news. If we found something sort of interesting we could pursue it. We could be more creative because we were doing a lot of features." Eden resigned to go into advertising in 1978. Today she is a public relations/marketing official for Creighton University. "The sad part as I look back is that I was so young and naive that I didn't recognize the opportunities around me."

THE TRANSFORMATION

By the mid-1970s women had become mainstream players in all Omaha newsrooms, and the transformation of the *World-Herald* Women's News Department was in progress. Eventually every anchor team included at least one woman, and women meteorologists reporting the weather are serious professionals, not sex symbols. Shannon's KETV news staff is about half women, and women cover all assignments in all types of conditions. Long gone are the days when the *World-Herald* was reluctant to send a woman to cover police or anything else. Similarly men write features for the Living section with no loss of masculinity or status.

The groundbreakers in Omaha news profiled here succeeded personally because they were outstanding journalists who sought only equal opportunity to excel in a field they loved and to prove they belonged. By working quietly behind the scenes, they became full partners in their newsrooms and opened formerly closed doors to their sex in addition to expanding the definition of what is newsworthy. So well did they succeed that female journalism students reading a book on the *New York Times* sex-discrimination lawsuit can scarcely believe such conditions once existed. Perhaps the best indication of the success of the baby boom women pioneer journalists is that hardly anyone in cities like Omaha even realizes that these pioneers ever successfully fought an important battle for equality.

By the late 1970s women journalists were no longer outsiders but rather were valuable members of their news teams. Women could cover any beat, holding jobs that women just ten years earlier only dreamed of, like anchoring TV newscasts. For the first time in the century in which Nebraska women had contributed greatly to journalism, their sex had ceased to be an issue, or at least much of an issue, except for obtaining jobs in top management.

Elia Peattie, Clara Bewick Colby, and Rheta Childe Dorr would have been delighted at the final outcome of their struggles for a place for women in journalism. The advertising cliché "You've come a long way baby" was true of Nebraska's women journalists and even more so for the cohort of women who followed. They anchored network news like Creighton alum Mary Alice Williams of CNN and headed the National Press Club in Washington (which once excluded women) like Mary Kay Quinlan, then of the *World-Herald*'s Washington bureau, now a journalism professor at the University of Nebraska–Lincoln. They led their news staffs like Deanna Sands, the *World-Herald*'s first woman managing editor, and Kathleen Rutledge of the *Lincoln Journal-Star*.

The greatest proof of the success of the groundbreakers is that current journalism students find their stories so difficult to believe. When some of them met Mary McGrath at an awards event and learned that they were talking to *the* Omaha woman who more than anyone else had opened doors to them, they were awed at encountering a legendary figure. In retrospect it is hard to overstate McGrath's influence on the opening of Omaha journalism to women. Not only was she one of the region's top journalists of either sex who had patiently waited for an opportunity to make full use of her gifts; she was also a role model for the baby boomers. Many of us were far less patient about how to make change, but we were smart enough to follow her lead. Mc-Grath helped restrain some of us from doing things we would later have regretted. Her wisdom helped make the long-term changes possible. She was the indispensable figure in the integration of women into all forms of media in Omaha.

Epilogue and Closing Thoughts

When I was first contemplating this project, a major male figure in Nebraska journalism warned me to be careful about claiming too much credit for my generation of women because there had always been women journalists in the state. I said nothing but thought, "You bet," chalking it up to male denial of the barriers we had broken. I'm glad now that I bit my tongue because he was right. I found that Nebraska had a rich history of women in journalism long before the baby boomers. The fact that I was unaware of this history speaks volumes about why regional research like this is so important. Ironically before undertaking this project, I had never been enamored of the women's history movement. I had no idea how many women of achievement in journalism and other fields have been overlooked even in state and regional histories where they might be expected to appear. I have found that women who were part of family enterprises have seldom received as much recognition as their husbands even when they have contributed equally to a news operation's success. As I have looked at the names in the Nebraska Press Association Hall of Fame, I think of women who should be added either for their individual achievements or recognized along with their husbands for their joint accomplishments. I hope that this book will encourage nominations of some of the women featured. Already the Nebraska Press Women's new female journalism Hall of Fame has recognized deserving women such as Bev Pollock, who logically should have shared her late husband's election to the NPA Hall of Fame.

If this project has taught me nothing else, it is that we cannot understand the history of women in the United States unless we consider local and regional dimensions because family obligations have limited the geographic and career mobility of the vast majority of American women. The nationally prominent women who typically are featured in the history of journalism and other fields are the exceptions. Many were so career driven that they sacrificed marriage and motherhood. This is understandable, but it fails to account for women of distinction who helped transform their towns like Ruth Best Pagel or who enjoyed satisfying career partnerships with their husbands like Pollock or who carved out careers around the needs of their families like Elia Peattie. When I think of how these women juggled the demands of careers and families in all eras, I feel a strong sense of sisterhood with them and a great satisfaction in telling their stories because during many of the prime years of my own career, I was juggling work and child rearing.

My encounter with the older women at Loyola University in Chicago also has deeply affected me, especially after reading the first chapter in Stephanie Coontz's *Strange Stirring* detailing the scope of the legal inequalities that women faced. I had known about many of the laws, bumped up against some of the discriminatory practices, and even contributed modestly to changing some others, but never quite understood how unequally women were treated until the social and legal changes of the 1970s. That reality makes the achievements of the women in this book and their peers in other fields elsewhere even more remarkable. I marvel at their courage and tenacity in the face of far greater odds for success than anything we baby boomers faced. We came of age at a time of tremendous momentum for change, part of a strong cohort of women who grew increasingly confident of success. We were a far cry from the lone women fighting for a place in the sun like many of the women profiled in this book or those I met in Chicago. I pray that this book will encourage such women to tell their stories so that their children and grandchildren can marvel at the odds they had to overcome. If we record these struggles, we are less likely to have to repeat them.

This project also has led me to ponder our society's definitions of success and achievement that value the national over the local or the regional, and the professional per se over the balance of personal and professional that so many of the women in this book exemplify. These women are wonderful role models for students because they illustrate a full spectrum of ways to be women of achievement. If this book helps unsung women all over the country in all fields celebrate their contributions and accomplishments, it would make the women I have written about very happy and delight me.

On a personal note this project has helped me celebrate my *own* career. Because both of my sisters had nationally significant careers and mine has unfolded entirely in Omaha, I have tended to compare my accomplishments unfavorably with theirs. I now realize that choosing a career in regional media that allowed me to be a daily presence in the lives of my two children was a wonderful decision that many remarkable women have shared. I realize that even if I had never been a mother and still chose work in Omaha and contribute to making it a better place, there would be nothing to apologize for.

Writing this book has been the richest professional experience of my life, a journey that has profoundly affected me as a person as well as a teacher and a writer. My fondest hope is that readers, too, will find affirmation of their lives, choices, and achievements in this celebration of Nebraska women in journalism no matter where they live or what they have done.

Notes

PREFACE

The Wisconsin colleague referenced early in the preface is Genevieve McBride of the University of Wisconsin–Milwaukee, who mentioned the wealth of potential subject material during a personal interview in Milwaukee, on July 19, 2010. The reaction to my research came from a presentation that I made during a speech at Loyola University's School of Communication on March 28, 2011. Information about the world before the women's movement came from a variety of sources, but I particularly recommend Stephanie Coontz's *Strange Stirring* and Gail Collins's *When Everything Changed*. Chapter 1 of Coontz is a superb and horrifying digest of the legal and social inequities that women faced prior to the changes of the early 1970s. I almost wish I could reprint it as an appendix to provoke readers to tell their own stories and to better understand the difficulties my subjects conquered to achieve what they did.

Maurine Beasley's assessment of the national significance of the work and the fact that no one had ever undertaken a project of this type before came in an e-mail that I received from her on July 2, 2010. A phone interview with Allen Beermann of the Nebraska Press Association provided excellent background on the culture of Nebraska and the role of women in Nebraska journalism that I relied on, although I did not quote his remarks.

INTRODUCTION

The material on the contrast in the *Omaha World-Herald* that I first encountered in 1969 versus the paper today is based on memories of my job interview there in April 1969 and a tour I took of the newsroom in April 2009 as I was preparing to write an initial proposal for this book. Much of the rest of the material relies on my memories of my life and career. Readers will have to trust that I am a reasonably good reporter. To prompt my memory of stories I had worked on, I went through some old *World-Herald* clippings that I accessed at the Douglas County Historical

Society Library. I learned about the *Farm Journal*'s launch of a national petition drive on women and farm inheritance in 1978 when I was working on my master's thesis, "Farm Women and the Media," and sought help with sources. When the editor I talked to heard my name and affiliation, she told me the outcome of their follow-up to my article on Doris Royal. An interview with Mary Heng-Braun, former head of the Omaha Community Foundation's Women's Fund, provided excellent background on the reasons that women seeking coverage of social and sex discrimination issues often turned to women reporters. Other interviews that helped me better understand my experiences and those of women in my generation included those with Cornelia Flora, Richard Shugrue, and Loree Bykerk. Flora, a distinguished scholar on midwestern women, offered excellent insights into the tactics that women like me used in our efforts to break down workplace barriers and why we employed such methods. Her insights and guidance on questions to ask interviewees were invaluable. My extensive interview with her as I began this project helped frame the entire book.

1. PIONEER WOMEN IN JOURNALISM

This chapter, especially the introductory remarks, relies heavily on Frederick Luebke's writings, especially his *Nebraska: An Illustrated History* and *The European Immigrants in the American West*. James C. Olson's *History of Nebraska* was the essential work on which I relied for information about what was happening in Nebraska throughout the various eras, the starting place for any author writing about Nebraska. Dorothy Weyer Creigh's *Nebraska* contains a number of useful insights about the state but is less comprehensive than Olson. The Cather quote is from Olson, *History of Nebraska*, 59.

The chapter relies heavily on overview books on women in the media for its foundational material about the national history of women in journalism. These include *Women, Men, and News*, by Paula Poindexter, Sharon Meraz, and Amy Schmitz Weiss and *Women and the Press*, by Patricia Bradley. Peggy A. Volzke Kelley's *Women of the Nebraska Hall of Fame* offered me my first list of names of noted Nebraska women journalists and was useful throughout this project. It was my best source on Harriet Dakin MacMurphy, for example. Ishbel Ross's *Ladies of the Press* is an excellent source on stunt girls and sob sisters. I also obtained background on sob sisters from Phyllis Abramson's *Sob Sister Journalism*. The Anne McCormick quote appears on page 27 of Downs's *Becoming Modern*.

The Nebraska State Historical Society (NSHS) provided sources for much of the remaining material on which this chapter is based. Patricia Gaster's article "Rosa Hudspeth and the Stuart Ledger, 1901–1907" furnished information for the profile on Hudspeth. Gaster, an archivist for NSHS, guided me to numerous smaller items in NSHS newsletters and county historical society newsletters from which I obtained the information about Nellie Bly and Maggie Mobley. Gaster also provided me with a long article on sob-sister journalist Ada Patterson from the October 1, 1908, issue of the *Crete News*. NSHS steered me to Elia Peattie's article on the early women of Nebraska journalism printed in Henry Allen Brainerd's *History of the Nebraska Press Association*. Finally, all articles from the *Evening World-Herald* issues cited were reviewed on microfilm that I accessed at Creighton University's Reinert Alumni Library (RAL). For this and many other chapters, Gaster and Andrea Failing of NSHS, as well as Beermann, were my starting places for names to explore. Mary Nash, reference librarian at Reinert, and Lynn Schneiderman of Interlibrary Loan at RAL also guided me to many sources.

2. THREE SUPERSTAR JOURNALISTS

The history of Elia Peattie relies on Susanne George Bloomfield's *Impertinences*, Catherine M. Downs's *Becoming Modern*, and Henry Allen Brainerd's *History of the Nebraska Press Association*. I determined that Peattie was not mentioned in the *Omaha World-Herald*'s centennial history, *A Century of Service 1885–1985*, by Hollis Limprecht, by both reading the entire book and checking the index of names.

The section on Willa Cather utilizes material included in Mildred R. Bennett's *World of Willa Cather* and Catherine Downs's *Becoming Modern*.

The portion of this chapter devoted to Clara Bewick Colby uses an entry listed by her name in the *Encyclopedia of the Great Plains*, edited by David J. Wishart; Ann Bausum's *Winning the Fight for a Woman's Right to Vote*; and an essay by E. Clair Jerry titled "The Role of Newspapers in the Nineteenth-Century Woman's Movement." I received guidance on Colby's life and suggestions on sources from Laureen Riedesel, director of the Beatrice Public Library.

All the news items cited near the conclusion of the chapter were from the *Woman's Tribune* and appeared between January 1, 1884, and July 7, 1888. I read all issues produced in Nebraska and accessed them on Nebraska State Historical Society microfilm.

3. THE PROGRESSIVE ERA

The brief history of the Progressive Era at the outset of this chapter utilizes source material from *The Golden Interlude, 1900–1910* and Ann Wiegman Wilhite's article "Sixty-Five Years Till Victory." As always I consulted Olson's previously referenced *History of Nebraska.*

The section focusing on Rheta Childe Dorr draws from Dorr's own books, *What Eight Million Women Want* and *A Woman of Fifty*; an article about her on Bookrags.com that I accessed on April 4, 2011; and a profile of her from Peggy A. Volzke Kelley's book *Women of the Nebraska Hall of Fame.* It also uses Patricia Bradley's *Women and the Press* and Zena Beth McGlashan's article "Club 'Ladies' and Working 'Girls': Rheta Childe Dorr and the New York Evening Post."

The historical information included in the subsection titled "The Fate of Most Women Journalists" draws on *Upstream Metropolis*, by Lawrence H. Larsen, Barbara J. Cottrell, Harl A. Dalstrom, and Kay Calame Dalstrom, and James C. Olson's *History of Nebraska.* The comparison of the Local Brevities and Social Whirl columns is based on material in the March 5, 1907, *Evening World-Herald* accessed in microfilm at Creighton University's Reinert Alumni Library.

The discussion of female photojournalists makes use of Martha Kennedy's article "Nebraska's Women Photographers."

The Social Whirl piece on the business leader's wedding appeared in the *Evening World-Herald* on November 5, 1912.

The information in "Women in the Weeklies" is based on an examination of twenty-five volumes of the Nebraska State Historical Society that record the ownership and management changes of virtually all newspapers ever published in the state.

4. WORLD WAR I

The discussion of World War I–era anti-German sentiment both in Nebraska and the United States that begins this chapter employs Jack W. Roger's article "The Foreign Language Issue in Nebraska, 1918–1923," and Paul Bartholomew's book *Leading Cases on the Constitution.*

The chapter text relies on my interview with Gilbert Savery, which took place in Lincoln, Nebraska, on August 7, 2009. It also makes use of Ida Clyde Clarke's book *American Women and the World War.* This important but obscure book, which I found almost by accident at Creighton's Reinert

Alumni Library, details the work of women in every state promoting the war under the auspices of state committees that reported to the federal Committee on Public Information (the Creel Committee), the national propaganda agency. It provides a fascinating, detailed look at the efforts to influence women through both local social coverage and the local foreign-language press. This book also documents local women at work for the Creel Committee. It has provided a tool for understanding the items from editions of the *Evening World-Herald*, the *Seward Tribune*, the *Cedar Bluffs Standard*, and the *Lincoln Star* that show women promoting the war. I accessed the *Evening World-Herald* on microfilm at Reinert Alumni Library, the *Lincoln Star* at Bennett Martin Public Library in Lincoln, and the *Seward Tribune* and *Cedar Bluffs Standard* on Nebraska State Historical Society microfilm.

The news items detailing female contributions to the war effort come from the *Evening World-Herald* ("Society Women Help Recruiters during Big Rush," March 28, 1917, and an untitled article appearing on March 29, 1917) and an untitled article in the *Lincoln Star* (March 8, 1917).

5. THE ROARING TWENTIES AND THE THIRTIES

The opening discussion, which details the struggles of Nebraskans during the difficult 1920s and 1930s, draws from Dorothy Weyer Creigh's *Nebraska* and James C. Olson's *History of Nebraska*. I accessed the University of Nebraska Athletic Department website for information about NU playing Notre Dame and obtained information about when various buildings in Omaha had been constructed from the Local History Department of the Omaha Public Library.

The subsection devoted to Bess Furman uses Furman's autobiography *Washington By-Line: The Personal History of a Newspaperwoman*; an article by Liz Watts concerning Furman, "Bess Furman, Nebraska's Front Page Girl: Her Formative Years"; Vicki L. Bagrowski's essay "Bess Furman 1894–1969"; and Ishbel Ross's *Ladies of the Press*.

The section about a "Fighting Woman Publisher" from Norfolk, Marie Weekes, uses Ishbel Ross's book as well. The passage concerning Mildred Heath is based mostly on an interview with her conducted by phone from Omaha on November 24, 2009. I obtained additional material on her from the articles "Silver Star Mildred Heath" on silverplanet.com (accessed November 24, 2009) and "There'll Always Be a Story to Tell" from bulletin. aarp.org (accessed November 24, 2009). I also drew information from

William Hull's *Dirty Thirties*. Allen Beermann of the Nebraska Press Association and Patricia Gaster of the Nebraska State Historical Society alerted me to Heath's story.

The segment regarding the birth of the University of Nebraska–Lincoln journalism department relies on the *University of Nebraska Bulletin* (1922–1923), John B. Thompson's *Political Scandal*, and Patricia Bradley's *Women and the Press*.

The radio portion draws from my phone interview with James Potter, completed in Omaha, Nebraska, on December 11, 2009, and Edith Abbott's "Crusade for Children: A Sister's Memories — Part III." Lynne Grasz of New York, who is profiled in chapter 8, informed me of Abbott's pioneering work in radio and introduced me to John Sorensen, who is editing this work.

The segment regarding the hard times endured by the journalism industry calls upon Betty Stevens's *30: A History of The Lincoln Journal*, Lois Scharf and Joan M. Jensen's *Decades of Discontent*, and David Kennedy's *Freedom from Fear*.

The news articles cited near the end of the chapter appeared in the *Omaha World-Herald* ("Woman Student at Nebraska Medical College Will Be Interne at Douglas County Hospital," July 4, 1926; "Business Women Will Enjoy Fourth," July 4, 1926; "Girls Rid Wheat Field of Parasites," July 4, 1926; "Miss Swartzlander of Library Staff to Wed," July 4, 1926; and a selection of untitled articles that appeared on July 5 and July 11, 1936). All were accessed on microfilm at Reinert Alumni Library. I read all issues of the Nebraska Press Association's newsletters for 1932 to obtain information on the impact of the Depression on weekly newspapers, especially those run by women, and found the information about Chattie Coleman Westinius of Stromsburg.

6. THE 1940S

The opening discussion detailing the events of the 1940s and the World War II struggle in Nebraska is based on material included in James C. Olson's *History of Nebraska*; Lawrence H. Larsen et al.'s *Upstream Metropolis*; "Reflection," an article appearing in *Nebraska History*; Esther Peterson's essay "Working Women"; D'Ann Campbell's *Women at War with America*; a letter from Kathleen Wirth to me dated March 22, 2010; and David Kennedy's *Freedom from Fear*.

The brief survey of opportunities afforded women statewide as a result of the war effort culls material from a news item by Betty Stevens, "Former

Photojournalist Keeps Busy in the Theater," in the March 20, 1988, *Sunday Journal Star*; Gilbert Savery's *As I Used To Say*; and an interview with Bonnie Reitan by the Lincoln County Historical Society in North Platte, Nebraska, January 11, 1999.

The segment concerning Marjorie Paxson comes from an interview by Diane K. Gentry that occurred on January 14, 1991, in Muskogee, Oklahoma, and is currently available online at the Washington Press Club's "Women in Journalism Project," http://www.wpcf.org/oralhistory/pax1 .html. I accessed the interview on January 12, 2010.

The portion devoted to Mae Eden utilizes a news item and a book by Betty Stevens: "Former Photojournalist Keeps Busy in the Theater" and *30: A History of The Lincoln Journal*, respectively. It also makes use of Eden's obituary in the *Lincoln Evening Journal*, "Mae Eden Lover of Theater etc.," March 21, 1996.

The portion of the chapter concerning Bonnie Reitan uses the interview with Reitan referred to earlier and Reitan's obituary in the *North Platte Telegraph*, "Goodfellow Shoe Fund Founding Member Dies," published April 8, 2003. The late Keith Blackledge, former editor of the *North Platte Telegraph*, referred me to the Lincoln County Historical Society for the information and sent me the obituary.

Betty Stevens's *30: A History of The Lincoln Journal* was the source of information about pay scales for women in Society versus men in Sports.

The discussion of Betty Craig uses Charlyne Berens's *Leaving Your Mark*. The information about Martha Bohlsen's career comes from Harold A. Soderlund's letter to the Nebraska Broadcasters Hall of Fame Selection Committee, received on November 12, 1986, along with some materials from her employers that were used to promote her shows and a video produced by Arlo Grafton, *Omaha Television: The Early Years* (1984)

The final portion of the chapter, detailing World War II's impact on local newspaper content, is the product of my interview with Alfred A. "Bud" Pagel in Lincoln, Nebraska, on January 22, 2010; letters about Ruth Best Pagel that he provided during that interview; and an interview with Emil Reutzel conducted by phone from Omaha, Nebraska, on March 3, 2010. I contacted Reutzel in Arizona with the assistance of his daughter Romney, a UNL classmate.

Two news items, "The Go Signal Is On for Christmas Parties," printed in the *Sunday World-Herald*, December 14, 1941, and "90 Year-Old-Woman Writes Song Predicting Jap Defeat," printed in the *Sunday World-Herald*,

December 14, 1941, were accessed through microfilm at Reinert Alumni Library. I found the other referenced news clips by examining microfilm of the *Lincoln Evening Journal* and the *Lincoln Star* at Bennett Martin Public Library in Lincoln and other editions of the *Omaha World-Herald* at Reinert Alumni Library. My general observations on the news treatment of women during the 1940s are based on my overall examination of selected editions in selected weeks of those papers, including those covering Pearl Harbor, D-Day, and the end of the war. I also explored some editions in 1946 and 1948 but found little worthy of comment.

7. THE 1950S

The discussion of the women in journalism in the fifties draws from material in Kay Mills's *Place in the News* and a selection of my interviews with Janet Pieper, Ruth Thone, and Beverly Pollock, all of which took place by phone from Omaha, Nebraska, on June 3, 12, and 14, 2010, respectively. It also utilizes a news item, "Bev Pollock Garners Top National Award," published in the *Nebraska Newspaper*, November–December 2002.

The section concerning Marianne Means, an NU graduate who covered President Kennedy, relies on a syndicated column by Means, "Until We Meet Again My Friends," printed in the *Wapakoneta Daily News* on October 10, 2008. The column appeared nationally, but the *Daily News* was the particular paper that appeared online when Creighton reference librarian Mary Nash discovered it during a search. I also Googled Means, obtained her entry in Who's Who, and examined a book that she wrote about first ladies, although it had no relevance to this project. I tried unsuccessfully to contact her for an interview.

The entry concerning Betty Craig Person Warner and her coverage of the Unicameral in Lincoln utilizes Charlyne Berens's book *Leaving Your Mark* and the obituary for Warner, "Funeral Services Set for Friday for Reporter, Civic Leader Warner," in the *Lincoln Star*, published on March 23, 1994.

The segment concerning women breaking barriers in both print and television media and the coverage of the Starkweather murders comes from my phone interviews with Patricia Wolfe (Omaha, Nebraska, April 23, 2010), Ninette Beaver (Omaha, Nebraska, June 10, 2010), and Dorothy Hayes Sater (Omaha, Nebraska, June 12, 2010). It also utilizes Ninette Beaver, B. K. Ripley, and Patrick Trese's *Caril*, as well as Earl Dyer's *Headline Starkweather* and Marj Marlette's obituary "Marj Marlette Dies; Ex-Journal Reporter," appearing in the *Lincoln Journal-Star* on November 6, 1999. I located Wolfe in Arizona with the help of retired *Omaha World-Herald* reporter Mary McGrath of Omaha, and Beaver in Arizona with the help of her former colleague David Hamer of Omaha.

8. THE 1960S

The introduction to chapter 8, concerning the Kennedys and the tumultuous 1960s, uses an article reporting on a famous speech by native Nebraskan Ted Sorensen titled "Education: Needle for Nebraska," which originally appeared in *Time* magazine on July 21, 1961, and is now available at http·//tinyurl.com/cadgwfk (accessed July 26, 2010). I also utilized James C. Olson and Ronald C. Naugle's *History of Nebraska* and Arthur M. Schlesinger Jr.'s *Robert Kennedy and His Times*. Information about the University of Nebraska during this period is based on my experiences there as a student between 1965 and 1968, including my participation in covering some of the issues mentioned for the *Daily Nebraskan* during AY 1966–67.

The portion of the chapter concerning Beverly Deepe and the Vietnam conflict uses my interview with Cornelia Flora (Ames, Iowa, April 9, 2009); Joyce Hoffmann's *On Their Own*; Beverly Deepe Keever's *Death Zones and Darling Spies*; an e-mail message from Beverly Deepe Keever (received June 12, 2010); and Beverly Keever's faculty biography authored by the University of Hawai'i School of Communications, available online at http://tinyurl.com/cnaomm5 (accessed August 2, 2010). Beverly Pollock of Ogallala drew Deepe to my attention when I interviewed Pollock for the chapter on the 1950s and asked if she could suggest other women from the era. Mary Nash of Reinert Alumni Library assisted me in finding the books featuring her.

The subsection detailing the education of women journalism students in the University of Nebraska system during the 1960s is the result of my interviews with Wilma Crumley (Lincoln, Nebraska, February 2, 2009), Carol Schrader (Omaha, Nebraska, July 7, 2010), and Cornelia Flora (Ames, Iowa, April 9, 2009). A personal note: Crumley was my lifelong mentor, and I conducted this interview during our final lengthy conversation before her death that May. See reference to the Flora interview in the introduction. My sister, Janet Poley of Lincoln, suggested interviewing Flora and helped me connect with her.

The portion of the chapter devoted to detailing the expanding roles for female journalists within local broadcasting draws from Gail Collins's

When Everything Changed; Billie V. Strand's thesis "The Role of Women in Nebraska Broadcasting," loaned to me by Larry Walklin of the University of Nebraska College of Journalism; my interview with Linda Beermann in Lincoln, Nebraska, on April 22, 2009; the Nebraska Broadcasters Association's Thirty-Ninth Annual Hall of Fame Awards Program (Lincoln, Nebraska, August 11, 2010); and an e-mail message from Janet Poley (received on July 24, 2010). Walklin, the leading authority on Nebraska broadcasting history, was an invaluable source of suggestions throughout this project on whom I relied for guidance in making interview selections. All errors of judgment are mine.

The chapter section regarding the advancement of women journalists within print media utilizes material from two phone interviews, with Janice Kreuscher (Omaha, Nebraska, July 25, 2010) and Elna Johnson (Omaha, Nebraska, July 26, 2010).

The segment about Lynne Grasz and Trudy Lieberman is the result of two e-mail messages from Grasz, received on December 8, 2009, and December 11, 2009, as well as my interview with her (August 2, 2010); Billie V. Strand's master's thesis, "The Role of Women in Nebraska Broadcasting"; Tom Nugent's article "Can She Quote You on That?"; and my phone interview with Trudy Lieberman (Omaha, Nebraska, August 2, 2010). Poley and many others suggested Grasz, who was very helpful with ideas overall for the project. Lieberman is a former classmate whom I connected with through the assistance of the University of Nebraska–Lincoln Alumni Association and the UNL College of Journalism.

The news item cited in the final segment of chapter 8 is "Respectable Spinsterhood Needed to Balance Census," which appeared in the *Omaha World-Herald* on May 7, 1961. I examined the issues and other articles referred to in this news coverage segment of the chapter on microfilm accessed at Reinert Alumni Library.

9. WOMEN JOURNALISTS OF COLOR

The discussion detailing the history of race relations in the Omaha area draws from Dennis C. Dickerson's *Militant Mediator*; Lawrence Larsen and Barbara J. Cottrell's *Gate City*; my phone interview with Cathy Hughes (Omaha, Nebraska, May 6, 2010); and a news item by Kent Sievers, "Omaha in Black and White: Poverty amid Prosperity," which appeared in the *Omaha World-Herald* on June 18, 2009.

The segment concerning Mildred Brown and the *Omaha Star* newspaper draws from Amy Helene Forss's "Mildred Brown Put Shine on Omaha Star"; my interview with Forss in Omaha, Nebraska, on April 22, 2010; and my phone interview with Cathy Hughes (Omaha, Nebraska, May 26, 2010). It also cites information from an e-mail from Patricia Gaster that I received on April 22, 2010, as well as two news items from the *Omaha Star*: the "Front Page Editorial" (July 11, 1966) and "The Impact of Wallace and the Aftermath" (March 7, 1968). I accessed all information from the *Omaha Star* using microfilm at Omaha's W. Dale Clark Public Library. Forss is an invaluable source for anyone seeking information about Brown. Ironically she had interviewed me earlier about Brown for this project because I could shed some light on Omaha during the early 1970s from my coverage of religion and race during the period.

The portion of the chapter devoted to Cheryl Parks Butler comes from my phone interview with Butler (Omaha, Nebraska, May 6, 2010); my phone interview with Cathy Hughes (Omaha, Nebraska, May 26, 2010); and an article by Chad Lorenz, "Complete Journalists from Nebraska Find Homes at the Post." I located Butler with assistance from Janice Kreuscher of Indianapolis and the University of Nebraska Alumni Association. Gilbert Savery, retired managing editor of the *Lincoln Evening Journal*, told me in an interview previously referenced that Butler was the first African American woman at the *Journal* and there were none at the *Omaha World-Herald*, the basis for my statement that she was the first of her race and sex to be part of a news staff of a major Nebraska newspaper. In searching for background on Butler, I also contacted Merrilee Miller in Omaha, a member of the Central High School Alumni Association.

The portion of the chapter regarding Eve Goodwin Christian and the diversification of the *Omaha World-Herald* staff uses material from Ralph Engleman's *Friendlyvision*, as well as my interview with Christian (Omaha, Nebraska, May 3, 2010). I obtained background information on African Americans at the *Omaha World-Herald* from James Clemon, former city editor and editorial page editor, in a personal interview in Omaha on April 6, 2009.

The last section on Cathy Hughes comes from my phone interview with her (Omaha, Nebraska, May 6, 2010) and an article by Jean Sanders, "Catherine Hughes" (accessed May 6, 2010). Alvin Goodwin of Omaha, brother of Eve Goodwin Christian, contacted Hughes on my behalf and arranged for the interview, which I would have had difficulty obtaining without such assistance.

10. INTEGRATING OMAHA MEDIA

The entirety of chapter 10 is the result of interviews that I conducted.

The beginning portion of the chapter, regarding Mary McGrath moving to the "cityside" at the *Omaha World-Herald*, comes from my interview with Robert Dorr in Omaha on April 3, 2009, and with McGrath in Omaha on July 3, 2010. The section on midwestern women and Equal Employment Opportunity laws and opportunities is the result of my phone interview with Scott Bosley in Omaha on April 2, 2009.

The portion regarding Omaha women and EEO law comes from my interviews with the following individuals: Loree Bykerk, Richard Shugrue, Cornelia Flora, and Carol Schrader between April 2009 and July 2010. Except for Flora, whom I interviewed in Ames, Iowa, the interviews were conducted in person or by phone from Omaha. I located Shugrue, a retired Creighton law professor, in Arizona with the assistance of the Creighton University School of Law. Bykerk is a professor of political science at the University of Nebraska at Omaha.

The section focusing on the biography of Mary McGrath comes from my interview with McGrath in Omaha on July 3, 2010. The segment on TV station interns and Rose Ann Shannon is the result of my interview with David Hamer in Omaha on April 6, 2009.

The entry on Carol Schrader comes from my interview with her in Omaha on July 7, 2010. Similarly, the piece on Rose Ann Shannon is from my interview with her, also in Omaha on July 8, 2010. The section on Ann Pedersen comes from my interview with her on July 8, 2010. I contacted Trina Creighton of the University of Nebraska–Lincoln College of Journalism and possibly the first female African American broadcast journalist in Omaha but discovered that she began her career later than the period of this study.

The subsection titled "Expanding the Definition of News" draws from interviews with Carol Schrader, Rose Ann Shannon, Robert Dorr, and David Hamer, all of whom have been previously cited in this note. I used background information from an interview with Mary Heng-Braun cited in the introduction but did not quote from it. It also utilizes material from my interview with Robyn Eden that took place in Omaha on June 29, 2009.

Bibliography

PUBLISHED SOURCES

Abramson, Phyllis. *Sob Sister Journalism*. New York: Greenwood Press, 1990.

Bagrowski, Vicki. "Bess Furman 1894–1969." In *Perspectives: Women in Nebraska History*, edited by Susan Pierce, 228–35. Lincoln: Nebraska Department of Education and Nebraska State Council for the Social Studies, 1984.

Bartholomew, Paul. *Leading Cases on the Constitution*. Totowa NJ: Littlefield, Adams, 1965.

Bausum, Ann. *Winning the Fight for a Woman's Right to Vote*. Washington DC: National Geographic Society, 2004.

Baxandall, Rosalyn, and Linda Gordon, eds. *America's Working Women*. New York: W. W. Norton, 1995.

Beasley, Maurine H., and Sheila J. Gibbons. *Taking Their Place*. Washington DC: American University Press, 1993.

Beasley, Maurine, and Sheila Silver. *Women in Media: A Documentary Source Book*. Washington DC: Women's Institute for Freedom of the Press, 1977.

Beaver, Ninette, B. K. Ripley, and Patrick Trese. *Caril*. Philadelphia: J. B. Lippincott, 1974.

Bennett, Mildred R. *The World of Willa Cather*. Lincoln: University of Nebraska Press, 1961.

Berens, Charlyne. *Leaving Your Mark*. Seward NE: Nebraska Times, 1997.

Bloomfield, Susanne George. *Impertinences*. Lincoln: University of Nebraska Press, 2005.

BookRags. "Encyclopedia of World Biography on Rheta Childe Dorr." http://www.bookrags.com/biography/rheta-childe-dorr.

Bradley, Patricia. *Women and the Press*. Evanston IL: Northwestern University Press, 2005.

Brainerd, Henry Allen. *History of the Nebraska Press Association.* Chicago: Inland Printer, 1923.

Breines, Winifred. *Young, White and Miserable.* Boston: Beacon Press, 1992.

Campbell, D'Ann. *Women at War with America.* Cambridge MA: Harvard University Press, 1984.

Charlton, Thomas, Lois Myers, and Rebecca Sharpless, eds. *Handbook of Oral History.* Lanham MD: AltaMira, 2006.

Clair, Jerry E. "The Role of Newspapers in the Nineteenth-Century Woman's Movement." In *A Voice of Their Own: The Woman Suffrage Press, 1840–1910,* edited by Martha M. Solomon, 113–28. Tuscaloosa: University of Alabama Press, 1991.

Clarke, Ida Clyde. *American Women and the World War.* New York: D. Appleton, 1918.

Clarke, Thurston. *The Last Campaign.* New York: Harry Holt, 2008.

Collins, Gail. *When Everything Changed.* New York: Little, Brown, 2009.

Coontz, Stephanie. *A Strange Stirring.* New York: Basic Books, 2011.

Copple, Neale. *Tower on the Plains.* Lincoln: Lincoln Sunday Journal and Star, 1959.

Creigh, Dorothy Weyer. *Nebraska.* New York: W. W. Norton, 1977.

Creswell, John. *Qualitative Inquiry and Research Design.* Thousand Oaks CA: Sage, 1998.

Curley, Edwin A. *Nebraska 1875: Its Advantages, Resources, and Drawbacks.* Lincoln: University of Nebraska Press, 2006.

Deutsch, Sarah Jane. *From Ballots to Breadlines.* New York: Oxford University Press, 1994.

Dickerson, Dennis C. *Militant Mediator.* Lexington: University Press of Kentucky, 1998.

Dorr, Rheta Childe. *What Eight Million Women Want.* Boston: Small, Maynard, 1910.

———. *A Woman of Fifty.* New York: Funk & Wagnalls, 1924.

Downs, M. Catherine. *Becoming Modern: Willa Cather's Journalism.* Selinsgrove PA: Susquehanna University Press, 1999.

Dyer, Earl. *Headline Starkweather.* Lincoln: Journal-Star Printing, 1993.

"Education Needle for Nebraska." *Time,* July 21, 1961, http://www.time .com/time/magazine/article/0,9171,897831,00.html.

Elwood-Akers, Virginia. *Women War Correspondents in the Vietnam War, 1961–1975.* Metuchen NJ: Scarecrow Press, 1988.

Engelman, Ralph. *Friendlyvision*. New York: Columbia University Press, 2009.

Forss, Amy. "Mildred Brown Puts Shine on Omaha Star." *The Reader*, August 21, 2008.

Furman, Bess. *Washington By-Line: The Personal History of a Newspaperwoman*. New York: Alfred A. Knopf, 1949.

Gaster, Patricia. "Rosa Hudspeth and the Stuart Ledger, 1901–1907." *Nebraska History* 79, no. 4 (Winter 1998): 171–78.

Greene, Bob. *Once Upon a Town*. New York: William Morrow, 2002.

Harvey, Brett. *The Fifties: A Women's Oral History*. New York: Harper Perennial, 1993.

Hecker, Eugene. *A Short History of Women's Rights*. Westport CT: Greenwood, 1971.

Hickman, Laura McKee. "Thou Shalt Not Vote." *Nebraska History* 80, no. 4 (Summer 1999): 55–65.

Hill, Jeff. *Women's Suffrage*. Detroit: Omnigraphics, 2006.

Hoffmann, Joyce. *On Their Own*. Philadelphia: DaCapo, 2008.

Huber, Joan, ed. *Changing Women in a Changing Society*. Chicago: University of Chicago Press, 1973.

Hull, William. *The Dirty Thirties*. Saint Paul: Minnesota Independent Publishers Association, 1989.

Hurt, R. Douglas. *The Great Plains during World War II*. Lincoln: University of Nebraska Press, 2008.

Iorio, Sharon Hartin, ed. *Qualitative Research in Journalism*. Mahwah NJ: Lawrence Erlbaum Associates, 2004.

Keever, Beverly Deepe. *Death Zones and Darling Spies: Seven Years of Vietnam War Reporting*. Lincoln: University of Nebraska Press, 2013.

Kelley, Peggy A. Volzke. *Women of the Nebraska Hall of Fame*. Omaha: Nebraska International Women's Year Coalition, 1976.

Kennedy, David. *Freedom from Fear*. New York: Oxford University Press, 1999.

Kennedy, Martha. "Nebraska's Women Photographers." *Nebraska History* 12, no. 2 (Summer 1991): 62–77.

Killian, Margaret. *Born Rich*. Omaha: Assistance League of Omaha, 1978.

Larsen, Lawrence, and Barbara J. Cottrell. *The Gate City*. Boulder CO: Pruett, 1982.

Larsen, Lawrence H., Barbara J. Cottrell, Harl A. Dalstrom, and Kay Calame Dalstrom. *Upstream Metropolis*. Lincoln: University of Nebraska Press, 2007.

Lief, Alfred. *Democracy's Norris.* New York: Octagon Books, 1977.

Limprecht, Hollis J. *A Century of Service, 1885–1985.* Omaha: Omaha World-Herald, 1985.

Lorenz, Chad. "Complete Journalists from Nebraska Find Homes at the Post." *University of Nebraska College of Journalism JNews Magazine,* Winter 2003, http://journalism.unl/edu/cojmc/alumni/jnews/0203-winter/post.shtml.

Luebke, Frederick, ed. *European Immigrants in the American West.* Albuquerque: University of New Mexico Press, 1998.

———. *Nebraska: An Illustrated History.* 2nd ed. Lincoln: University of Nebraska Press, 2005.

Madison, James R., ed. *Heartland.* Bloomington: Indiana University Press, 1988.

McGlashan, Zena Beth. "Club 'Ladies' and Working 'Girls': Rheta Childe Dorr and the New York Evening Post." *Journalism History,* Spring 1981, 7–13.

———. "Women Witness the Russian Revolution: Analyzing Ways of Seeing." *Journalism History,* Summer 1985, 54–61.

Means, Marianne. "Until We Meet Again, My Friends." Hearst syndicated column, October 10, 2008.

Miller, Douglas T. *The Fifties: The Way We Really Were.* Garden City NY: Doubleday, 1977.

Mills, Kay. *A Place in the News.* New York: Dodd, Mead, 1988.

Murphy, Lucy Eldersveld, and Wendy Hamand Venet, eds. *Midwestern Women: Work, Community, and Leadership at the Crossroads.* Bloomington: University of Indiana Press, 1997.

Nielsen, Margaret. "The Girl Who Interviewed Nellie Bly." *Buffalo Tales,* February 1979, 1–2.

Norris, George. *Fighting Liberal.* New York: MacMillan, 1945.

Nugent, Tom. "Can She Quote You on That?" *Nebraska Magazine,* Summer 2010, 27–29.

Olson, James C. *History of Nebraska.* Lincoln: University of Nebraska Press, 1955.

Olson, James C., and Ronald C. Naugle. *History of Nebraska.* 3rd ed. Lincoln: University of Nebraska Press, 1997.

Omaha Times Remembered. Omaha: Omaha World-Herald, 1999.

Otis, Harry, and Donald Erickson. *E Pluribus Omaha.* Omaha: Lamplighter Press, 2000.

Peters, Sharon L. "There'll Always Be a Story to Tell." *AARP Bulletin Today*, September 30, 2008, http://aarp.org/bulletin.

Peterson, Esther. "Working Women." In *The Woman in America*, edited by Robert Jay Lifton, 144–72. Boston: Houghton Mifflin, 1964.

Peterson, M. Jeanne. *Family, Love, and Work in the Lives of Victorian Gentlewomen.* Bloomington: University of Indiana Press, 1989.

Pierce, Susan, ed. *Perspectives: Women in Nebraska History.* Lincoln: Nebraska Department of Education and Nebraska State Council for the Social Studies, 1984.

Pipher, Mary. *The Middle of Everywhere.* New York: Harcourt, 2002.

Poindexter, Paula, Sharon Meraz, and Amy Schmitz Weiss, eds. *Women, Men, and News.* New York: Routledge Taylor & Francis Group, 2008.

Poitier, Sidney. *The Measure of a Man.* New York: HarperSanFrancisco, 2000.

Potter, James E. "Barkley vs. Pool. Woman Suffrage and the Nebraska Referendum Law." *Nebraska History* 69, no. 1 (Spring 1988): 11–18.

Randolph, Ladette, and Nina Chevchuk-Murray, eds. *The Big Empty.* Lincoln: University of Nebraska Press, 2007.

"Reflection." *Nebraska History* 72 (Winter 1991): 242–50.

Ritchie, Donald A. *Doing Oral History.* Oxford: Oxford University Press, 2003.

Roberts, Cokie. *We Are Our Mothers' Daughters.* New York: Perennial, 1998.

Rogers, Jack W. "The Foreign Language Issue in Nebraska, 1918–1923." *Nebraska History* 39 (March 1958): 1–22.

Ross, Ishbel. *Ladies of the Press.* New York: Harper & Brothers, 1936.

Sanders, Jean. "Catherine Hughes: A Pioneer Radio Entrepreneur." Nebraska State Education Association, http://nsea.org/news/hughesprofile.htm.

Savery, Gil. *As I Used To Say.* Lincoln: Aluminum Pica Pole Press, 2002.

Scharf, Lois. *To Work and to Wed.* Westport CT: Greenwood, 1980.

Scharf, Lois, and Joan M. Jensen. *Decades of Discontent.* Boston: Northeastern University Press, 1987.

Schlesinger, Arthur M., Jr. *Robert Kennedy and His Times.* Boston: Houghton Mifflin, 1978.

Severin, Werner J., and James W. Tankard Jr. *Communication Theories.* 5th ed. New York: Addison Wesley Longman, 2001.

Shortridge, James R. *The Middle West: Its Meaning in American Culture.* Lawrence: University Press of Kansas, 1989.

Smith, Karen Manners. *New Paths to Power*. New York: Oxford University Press, 1994.

Solomon, Martha M., ed. *A Voice of Their Own*. Tuscaloosa: University of Alabama Press, 1991.

Sorel, Nancy Caldwell. *The Women Who Wrote the War*. New York: Arcade, 1999.

Sorensen, John, ed. "The Crusade for Children" by Edith Abbott. Segment from unpublished book.

Stevens, Betty. *30: A History of the Lincoln Journal*. Henderson NE: Service Press, 1999.

Strand, Billie V. "The Role of Women in Nebraska Broadcasting." Master's thesis, University of Nebraska, 1981.

Stuhr Museum of the Prairie Pioneer Research Department. "Hall County's Pioneering Women." March 1, 2000. http://www .stuhrmuseum.org/research/womenbus.htm.

Thompson, John B. *Political Scandal*. Cambridge: Polity Press, 2000.

Time-Life Books. *The Clamorous Era, 1910–1920*. This Fabulous Century. New York: Time-Life Books, 1969.

———. *The Golden Interlude, 1900–1910*. This Fabulous Century. New York: Time-Life Books, 1969.

Thone, Ruth Raymond. *Women and Aging*. New York: Haworth, 1992.

Watts, Liz. "Bess Furman, Nebraska's Front Page Girl: Her Formative Years." *Nebraska History* 74, no. 1 (Summer 1993): 63–71.

Weiland, Matt, and Sean Wilsey, eds. *State by State*. New York: HarperCollins, 2008.

Whitt, Jan. *Women in American Journalism*. Urbana: University of Illinois Press, 2008.

Wilhite, Ann Wiegman. "Sixty-Five Years Till Victory." *Nebraska History* 49, no. 2 (June 1968): 149–63.

Winfield, Betty Houchin, ed. *Journalism, 1908*. Columbia: University of Missouri Press, 2008.

Wishart, David J., ed. *Encyclopedia of the Great Plains*. Lincoln: University of Nebraska Press, 2004.

Wolbrecht, Christina. *The Politics of Women's Rights*. Princeton NJ: Princeton University Press, 2000.

Yin, Robert K. *Case Study Research*. 2nd ed. Thousand Oaks CA: Sage, 1994.

Yow, Valerie Raleigh. *Recording Oral History*. 2nd ed. Walnut Creek CA: AltaMira, 2005.

INTERVIEWS BY AUTHOR

Beasely, Maurine. Noted women's journalism historian. E-mail of July 2, 2010.

Beaver, Ninette. Retired reporter/producer, KMTV. June 10, 2010.

Beermann, Allen. Executive director, Nebraska Press Association. July 12, 2010.

Beermann, Linda. Former reporter/weathercaster, KOLN-TV. April 22, 2009.

Bosley, Scott. Director, American Society of Newspaper Editors. April 2, 2009.

Butler, Cheryl Parks. Retired recruitment director, *Washington Post*. May 6, 2010.

Bykerk, Loree. Professor of political science, University of Nebraska at Omaha. April 7, 2009.

Christian, Eve Goodwin. Former reporter, *Omaha World-Herald*. May 3, 2010.

Clemon, James. Retired editorial page editor, *Omaha World-Herald*. April 6, 2009.

Crumley, Wilma. Professor emerita, University of Nebraska–Lincoln College of Journalism. February 2, 2009.

Dorr, Robert. Retired reporter and editor, *Omaha World-Herald*. April 3, 2009.

Flora, Cornelia. Professor of sociology, Iowa State University. April 9, 2009.

Forss, Amy. Professor of history, Metropolitan Community College. April 21, 2010.

Grafton, Arlo. Omaha video photographer and editor. March 15, 2010.

Grasz, Lynne. President, Grasz Communications. August 2, 2010.

Hamer, David. Retired photographer, WOW-TV, KMTV, and KETV. April 6, 2009.

Heath, Mildred. Columnist, *Overton Beacon-Observer*. November 24, 2009.

Heng-Braun, Mary. Former head of the Omaha Community Foundation's Women's Fund. July 2, 2010.

Hughes, Cathy. Chairwoman of the board, Radio One. May 26, 2010.

Johnson, Elna. Copublisher, *Imperial Republican*. July 26, 2010.

Keever, Beverly Deepe. Retired professor of journalism, University of Hawai'i. E-mail response to questions, June 12, 2010.

Kreuscher, Janice, JD. Former editor, *Lincoln Evening Journal.* July 25, 2010.

Lieberman, Trudy. Contributing editor, *Columbia Journalism Review.* August 2, 2010.

McBride, Genevieve. Professor, University of Wisconsin–Milwaukee. July 19, 2010.

McGrath, Mary. Retired reporter, *Omaha World-Herald.* July 3, 2010.

Pagel, Alfred, Jr. Professor of journalism, University of Nebraska–Lincoln. January 22, 2010.

Pedersen, Ann. Former reporter/news executive, WOWT. July 8, 2010.

Pieper, Janet. Former cabinet member for Governor Charley Thone and staff member of California Polytechnical Institute. E-mail response to questions, June 13, 2010.

Poley, Janet. Executive director, ADEC. E-mail response to questions, July 24, 2010.

Pollock, Beverly. Retired copublisher, *Keith County News.* June 14, 2010.

Potter, James. Senior research historian, Nebraska State Historical Society. December 11, 2009.

Reutzel, Emil. Retired editor, *Norfolk Daily News.* March 2, 2010.

Sater, Dorothy Hayes. Retired Omaha journalist and PR executive. June 12, 2010.

Savery, Gilbert. Retired managing editor, *Lincoln Journal.* August 7, 2009.

Schrader, Carol. Former anchor, KETV. July 7, 2010.

Shannon, Rose Ann. News director, KETV. July 9, 2010.

Shugrue, Richard. Professor emeritus, Creighton University Law School. April 1, 2009.

Thone, Ruth Raymond. Columnist and author from Lincoln. June 12, 2010.

Walklin, Larry. Professor of journalism, University of Nebraska–Lincoln. November 13, 2009.

Waters, Patricia. Retired Living section editor, *Omaha World-Herald.* April 23, 2009.

Wolfe, Patricia. Retired Living section editor, *Omaha World-Herald.* April 23, 2010.

CPSIA information can be obtained at www.ICGtesting.com
Printed in the USA
BVOW071623030313

314540BV00001B/1/P